Here is a sane guide ⬚⬚⬚⬚⬚ ⬚⬚
Jonathan Gould is b ⬚⬚⬚⬚⬚ d
a loving concern for ⬚⬚⬚⬚⬚ ;
answers to important
chapter. I have seen ⬚⬚⬚⬚⬚ ⬚⬚⬚ ⬚⬚⬚ out of fog
into faith under his ministry and hope this book will
bring many more.

Simon Manchester
Senior Minister,
St Thomas' Anglican Church, Sydney, Australia

What Christians Believe is material regularly used by
Jonathan Gould as an introductory course for newcomers,
believers and unbelievers. It has long proved its worth
for those willing to think. Warmly recommended for
similar use and for the church bookstall.

Dick Lucas
Formerly Rector,
St Helens Bishopsgate, London

This book did my head and my heart a lot of good!
I found real clarity for my mind and a renewed desire to
know and serve the Christ in whom Christians believe.

Rico Tice
Author, *Christianity Explored* and Associate Minister,
All Souls Church, Langham Place, London

These days, Christians are all too often known only
for things like their politics, their social views, or their
music. But what we should be known for is the quality of
our lives and the content of our belief. Jonathan Gould
has done us a tremendous service by outlining in clear
strokes *What Christians Believe*. With respect and insight
into the real questions people ask, Gould explains what
the Bible has to say about God, human beings, Jesus

Christ, and faith. With unapologetic pastoral clarity, Gould reminds us that Christianity is not about religious sensibilities added on to an otherwise worldly life, but about radically God-centered truth that completely reorganises our lives for his glory. The result of these two concerns is that this is a book for anyone who not only wants to know what Christians believe, but why that belief matters. I cannot recommend it highly enough.

Michael Lawrence
Senior Pastor,
Hinson Baptist Church, Portland, Oregon

I have been wanting a book that simply and clearly explains basic Christian beliefs. We do not want to be spoken down to and supplementary questions need to be tackled relevantly and honestly. *What Christians Believe* is exactly what we have been looking for. I shall not hesitate to pass it on to thoughtful and enquiring friends.

Jonathan Fletcher
Minister,
Emmanuel Church, Wimbledon, London

This book is like journeying with a wise and knowledge-able tour guide. It is concerned with the interests of the traveller, answering them in a deep and wide manner while being absolutely true to what is being observed. The guide then moves the group safely to the final destination – the best of all destinations.

Archie Poulos
Head of Ministry Department,
Moore College, Sydney, Australia

What Christians Believe

Jonathan Gould

Copyright © Jonathan Gould 2012

paperback ISBN 978-1-84550-922-4
epub ISBN 978-1-78191-069-6
mobi ISBN 978-1-78191-070-2

Published in 2012
by
Christian Focus Publications
Geanies House, Fearn, Ross-shire,
IV20 1TW, Scotland.

www.christianfocus.com

Cover design by DUFI-ART.com

Printed by
Bell and Bain, Glasgow

Contents

Preface

I well remember living much of the first two decades of my life in a spiritual fog. It wasn't that I was an 'unbeliever'; I just didn't know what I believed. And such experience as I had of church and Christians, and such exposure as I had to the message of the Bible, had not yet shed sufficient light on my path to pierce through that fog.

But during my time at university some of that fog lifted as I met Christians who, by the lives they lived and by the teaching they gave, opened me up to listen and to understand 'what Christians believe'. In the decade that followed, during which I studied law and practised with a City of London law firm, these Christian convictions strengthened.

In the two decades since then as a church minister, first and briefly in Sydney, Australia, and then at St John's in Downshire Hill in London, I have played a part in helping others out of that same kind of spiritual fog that I experienced. And where individuals have been helped, it has been through that same combination of lives lived in a God-honouring way and clear teaching about 'what Christians believe'. The first of these 'helps' – the attractiveness of Christians' lives – cannot be presented on a printed page, but you may know of Christians whose lives inspire you to know what inspires them. The second of these 'helps', the clear presentation of what Christians believe, I have tried to provide through a short course originally held over four evenings. The content of that short course forms the basis of what you hold in your hands now.

We begin by looking at what God is like, and why God has made us (ch. 1). We go on to look at some common mistakes we tend to make about God and how to relate to God (ch. 2). We then look at the person of Jesus and what is claimed by him and for him (ch. 3). We also consider, in chapter 4, how matters of 'faith' relate to matters of 'fact'. At the centre of the course, and of this book, are the twin questions of 'What's gone wrong with the world?' (ch. 5) and 'Does God care?' (ch. 6). Then, on the central issue 'How can I know God?' we listen first to one of the Bible's own talks, given by an early preacher (ch. 7) and second to Jesus in conversation with a man called Nicodemus (ch. 8). Finally, chapter 9 is the story of one man who received new life from Christ. I include this to show that the message of this book, like the message of the Bible, is not just information, it is an invitation.

It *is* information about the God the Bible tells us is there. But more than that, it is an *invitation* to submit to that God, and receive with joy the new life he gives. This book is likely to be most useful to you if you are able to read it with the attitude, 'God, if you are there and if you have things to say to me, help me to hear them and respond in the way you desire.'

Preface

You may read this book as a Christian wanting a refresher course. Or you may read this as someone who is interested without necessarily regarding yourself as committed. If either of these describes you, I have written with you in mind.

I should add there are two assumptions underlying all that follows. The first is that we discover what Christians believe by understanding another book – or collection of books – which is the Bible. And therefore each chapter is an attempt to clarify a key aspect of what Christians believe by looking at a passage of the Bible. There are, of course, other ways of ascertaining what Christians believe; one would be to ask Christians today what they believe, and another would be to read the published works of Christians of previous generations. But both those ways of investigating Christian belief would take you beyond themselves to the source of authority for what they believe – the Bible. I am seeking to go straight to that authoritative source for a quick and sure answer to what Christians believe – a source which you can check for yourself.

The second assumption I am making is that the Bible is reliable in all that it teaches. Except for a short postscript, no attempt is made to defend its reliability. In my experience the issue of the Bible's reliability can detain too many for too long. Scrutinizing the messenger delays the process of listening to the message and in practice many of us never get to listen to the message because, we think, we are not sure about the messenger. But this is an unnecessary delay. If there is indeed such a God as Christians believe, who has indeed caused the Bible to be written by the hands of many human authors, is that same God not well able to convince us of the Bible's truthfulness as we read?

9

If in the end we are not convinced by the message, it is illogical and improbable to suppose that any human argument or further evidence for the divine inspiration of these Scriptures will convince us.

One potential problem in what follows is that you will not get the opportunity to ask the questions on your mind as you would if we walked and talked together. It is not a total solution, but at the close of each chapter, and based on the questions frequently asked on the course, I am going to imagine two characters called 'Jack' and 'Jill' asking the kind of questions you might voice. Though better known for 'going up a hill to fetch a pail of water', I hope Jack and Jill can serve a useful purpose in asking (some of) your questions and relaying to you some of my answers.

1 God and man

Christianity, if false, is of no importance, and if true, of infinite importance. The one thing it cannot be is moderately important.

C.S. LEWIS

Investigating the Christian faith is a hazardous business. We may begin our investigation in an open frame of mind, prepared to find much in the faith that is inspiring and uplifting, as well as a certain amount about which we remain unconvinced.

However, in the end, we can only reach one of two verdicts concerning the enormous claims that Christianity makes. Either we shall conclude that it is true or that it is false. And our lives will bear out our verdict. If it is false, then there is an end of the matter. We may safely put Bible and church with their doctrinal fictions on one side, and ignore the personal constraints and cultural expectations that flow from them.

If, however, Christianity is true, the enormity of its claims means everything will change for us. The purpose of our lives will change and with that we will have a whole new basis for evaluating the priority and importance of all that we might do. 'Christianity' cannot simply be the bit that we tack on to otherwise busy and fulfilling lives directed by some other inner guiding light. No; if

Christianity is true, then the God of which it speaks must be central to life and my purpose in living.

A psalm (or a song) of King David, the most famous of Israel's kings, written in about 1000 B.C., speaks of the God who is there and the purpose for which he has made us:

> [1]O LORD, our Lord, how majestic is your name in all the earth!
>
> You have set your glory above the heavens.
> [2]From the lips of children and infants you have ordained praise because of your enemies, to silence the foe and the avenger.
>
> [3]When I consider your heavens, the work of your fingers, the moon and the stars, which you have set in place,
> [4]what is man that you are mindful of him, the son of man that you care for him?
> [5]You made him a little lower than the heavenly beings and crowned him with glory and honour.
>
> [6]You made him ruler over the works of your hands; you put everything under his feet:
> [7]all flocks and herds, and the beasts of the field,
> [8]the birds of the air, and the fish of the sea, all that swim the paths of the seas.
>
> [9]O LORD, our Lord, how majestic is your name in all the earth! (Ps. 8)[1]

WHAT IS GOD LIKE?

What is God like, according to King David? The short answer given in a word, both at the beginning and end of this psalm, is that God is 'majestic': 'how majestic is your name in all the earth' (v. 1, 'name' here standing for the whole character of the God of whom he speaks).

---

1   For a list of abbreviations for Scripture, see p. 223.

David was himself a great king, and this word 'majestic' might well have been used to describe himself and his position in the land he ruled. In relation to royalty, the word 'majestic' speaks of power and splendour.

But, more than that, the God to whom he ascribes such majesty is no mere local and tribal deity. This God is not hidden away in the obscurity of just one small place. No, this God has made his 'name' known 'in all the earth' – that is to all people in every place. The truth about God is not gleaned with great difficulty by brilliant academics in ivory towers, drenched in learning and a pile of ancient languages. Here is truth accessible in the remotest parts of our planet Earth, to every people group in our world.

This truth about God is revealed primarily through the splendour of our universe. King David has done an easy thing and taken a walk outside on a clear moonlit night. He has lifted up his eyes to the skies. He stops to consider the immensity and the beauty of the universe he can see, and finds that it declares the God who is behind it all – the God who made it all and who owns it all. The heavens King David sees are the Lord's: '*your* heavens, the work of *your* fingers', he says. The moon and the stars – *you*, Lord, have set them in place (v. 3).

It will be clear that a reliable Bible – such as we are assuming – is not to be interpreted with wooden literalism. To speak of God's 'fingers' or 'hands' is not to say that God is a man up there with eyes, ears, a nose and two hands with four fingers and a thumb on each. This is anthropomorphic language – in other words language which is personal, physical and human ('hands' and 'fingers') is being used to communicate the truth about God's creative activity in making the world.

And the truth is this universe is not an accident; it is a creation and this creation reveals its creator. It is as though stamped across the sky are the words 'Made by

God' or, more accurately, 'Made by Me'. For the heavens are not simply attributed by man to God, in the absence of some more thoughtful scientific explanation. The heavens are God's handiwork, and their magnificence reveals the majesty of their maker to us. And the majesty of God, both his awesome power and his unutterable splendour, that he publishes 'above the heavens' (v. 1) is for all to see. The universe is *God's* testimony to himself, and his primary means of revealing himself to all of humanity: 'How *majestic* is your name... *in all the earth.'*

SOMETHING OR SOMEONE?

And yet this language of fingers and hands tells us more than that the creator God is powerful. This God, of whom King David speaks, is not only powerful to create, but is personal too. David speaks of '*your* glory', '*your* heavens', 'the moon and the stars which *you* have set in place', 'the work of *your* fingers' and the 'works of *your* hands'. And more than all these, King David speaks of God's *name*: 'How majestic is your *name* in all the earth.'

Quite unlike the way we might use 'O God!' as an exclamation or in the heat of a moment to express frustration or annoyance, King David's 'O LORD' is a reverent address of God using the name by which he has revealed himself in history.[2] So for King David to

---

2   The particular episode of the history of God's people that is in mind here concerns God's call of Moses from relative obscurity (and a kind of self-imposed exile) to the leadership of God's people, chronicled in Exodus chs. 3-4. Specifically, he was to lead them out of slavery in Egypt to the land God had long since promised to give them. Moses, half doubting his call, and wondering if he will ever be able to convince his fellow Israelites of his God-given authority, turns to God and says 'Suppose I go to the Israelites and say to them, "The God of your fathers has sent me to you," and they ask me, "What is his name?" Then what shall I tell them?' In reply God says 'I AM WHO I AM. This is what you are to say to the Israelites: "I AM has sent me to you"' (Exod. 3:13-14). The Hebrew for LORD sounds like the Hebrew for I AM.

address God as 'LORD' (printed in capitals in our Bibles), is not simply to give God a title of honour (Sir, Dr, Rev., etc.) but to address God using this name – LORD – by which he has revealed himself. By itself all the talk of God's power in creation could conjure up notions of impersonal forces. But God has made himself known not only through nature, but by the giving of his name. God has revealed himself not only by acts of power in creation, but by words of personal communication.

According to the record, God revealed himself to certain people, described as the fathers of the Israel-ite people: Abraham, Isaac and Jacob, and then subsequently to others (including Moses). Through this revelation made to these men, and passed on by them to subsequent generations, God was able to call a people to belong to himself. By the time King David writes, this is the reality; there is a people that belongs to this God – the Israelite people. To use the language of this psalm, 'the LORD' (that is, God's name) has become *their* 'Lord' (that is, *their* acknowledged ruler or king). So the psalmist can begin and end this song identifying the God to whom he speaks 'O LORD, *our* Lord' [my italics].

This all-powerful and utterly personal God who historically called a people, descendants of Abraham, to belong to himself, is the same creator God who today calls people from among all the nations to belong to him. A god that was all-powerful, but not personal, could compel us to fear it (rather as one might fear the power of the sea), but could not create the possibility of any sort of relationship. On the other hand, a god who was personal, but not the all-powerful creator, might collect some friends, but could not command our allegiance. By contrast to these half-truths, the God of the Bible, majestic in power and personal in character, both creates the possibility of relationship with him

15

and, rightly, commands the allegiance of all those to whom he speaks.

This revelation of God as all-powerful and yet utterly personal means that it is really impossible to be indifferent to him. In the end, there will be those who gladly praise the Lord God and those who oppose him. But face-to-face with the Lord God, spiritual neutrality is not an option in this life or indeed the next.

Not only is God's self-revelation something we need to consider with great care, knowing just how high the stakes are, but this fundamental truth that the powerful creator of the universe is personal and knowable, supplies a key to two further truths in this psalm concerning mankind and the purpose for which God made us.

MADE IN GOD'S IMAGE

The first truth, quite astonishingly, is that God made us to be like him. The very same word that the psalm uses to speak of God's splendour and majesty, namely 'glory' ('You have set your *glory* above the heavens' v. 1), is now the word used to describe mankind: 'You made him a little lower than the heavenly beings and crowned him with *glory* and honour' (v. 5). It's clearly not coincidental; we are being told that men and women were made to be like their maker. We find this truth taught in the account of creation in Genesis, the first book of the Bible, in the words 'Let us make man in our image, in our likeness', and then again in the words 'So God created man in his own image, in the image of God he created him; male and female he created them' (Gen. 1:26-27).

One consequence of this truth is that we can learn something about God by looking at mankind. But a second important consequence is that we learn what we were made to be like by looking at God. God's *glory* is, at least in some respects, to be the model for our own. The God of *glory* has crowned mankind that he has made with *glory*. Or to use the language of Genesis, God has made us in his image, in his likeness, and therefore he supplies in his very own nature and character the pattern to which you and I were made to conform.

Here is the answer to the perennial question 'Who am I?' This question sends many of us on a far-reaching, but ultimately fruitless, quest to discover our real inner selves. But the answer is not found by looking in at ourselves; it is found by looking *outside* of ourselves at the creator God who made us to be like him, that is, to reflect his glory.

We do not now reflect God's glory as fully as he intended, for reasons we shall see in a later chapter. But the restoration of my true purpose and dignity, reflecting the glory of the God who made me, comes about through belonging to the LORD, as my Lord, and through a personal relationship with him.

This truth has some small parallel in our human relationships because we tend to become like those whose company we keep. To observers, husbands and wives can grow to be like one another; children can become like their parents ('like father, like son' or 'a chip off the old block'); peers exercise a phenomenal influence over one another for good or ill ('peer pressure'); and friends of all ages unconsciously imitate one another. The old adage that 'you can tell a man by the company he keeps' reflects this same truth, as does its biblical equivalent that 'bad company corrupts good character.'

And what we observe in human experience finds its corollary in spiritual terms; if humanity is to reflect deity, humanity must relate to deity. A reflection of God, and a restoration of his image in us, will depend on a relationship with God. If we are to find ourselves, we must know our creator because the real me was made to be like the real God. To be able to say that *the* LORD is *our* Lord, is ultimately the way in which his glory will, once again, crown our lives.

MADE TO RULE

The other surprising truth we see here, concerning the purpose for which God made man, is that God has given mankind a task to perform. God made mankind to look after this world for him:

> 6You made him ruler over the works of your hands; you put everything under his feet:
> 7all flocks and herds, and the beasts of the field, 8the birds of the air, and the fish of the sea, all that swim the paths of the seas (Ps. 8:6-8).

To speak of God as maker is true as far as it goes, but it does not go far enough if we conclude that God, having made the world, has put his feet up for an eternally long weekend, or that he is off on another new project. No, the world God has made is a world which he continues to rule. But for the most part the way in which God exercises his benevolent rule of his world is by entrusting it to our care. God says to mankind – you rule over the plant and animal kingdoms.

The first book of the Bible, Genesis, tells us that God put a man and a woman in a garden, and commissioned them to work it and take care of it. It's a big task, and an even bigger one to carry out responsibly, as environmental campaigners frequently remind us. For the commission to rule over the world, both its animal and plant life, is not an excuse to plunder the world's resources recklessly, and pollute what we don't consume. Nor is it permission to be idle whilst the needs of our fellow men and women across the world are left fatally neglected and the world's resources carelessly underexploited. God has given to humanity the resources that are needed to care and provide for human life and exercise a responsible care for the animal kingdom. It is a solemn trust.

Surely this is not easily accomplished. And man's God-given ingenuity has proved to be a double-edged sword. At its best, it exhibits great creativity, and the agricultural, scientific and technological endeavours of the three thousand years since King David wrote his psalm testify that mankind has some ability to fulfil this high calling. But the evidence is not all one way. According to the book of Genesis, when God finished each aspect of his creation, 'God saw that it was good.' The evidence today is more mixed than that. There has not always been the benevolent care and rule over the animal kingdom that is worthy of the good creator's perfectly good creation. And much that people suffer in this world has a reason other than a real lack of physical resources to supply the want. For example, Burma is a country so fertile that it used to be known as the 'rice bowl of Asia', yet, not long ago, one in three of its children were malnourished, according to the World Food Programme. In 2000, *The Economist* declared Burma the 'most needlessly miserable country'.[3] Since then conditions have got much worse.

In a recent and salutary reminder, Lord Rees (Astronomer Royal and President of the Royal Society) wrote 'our planet has existed for 45 million centuries. But this century is the first in which one species – ours – could threaten the entire biosphere.'[4]

These sorts of statistics highlight the immense task which, under God, is ours. Only a breathtaking arrogance

---

3   *The World in 2000* (Special issue of *The Economist*), p. 43.

4   *The Times*, 'Nobel Laureate Symposium' 26.5.09.

on our part would say that this God-given task could be fulfilled without God-given resources of love and wisdom – the will to care and the ability to provide. All this is a sure sign that relating rightly *to* God is the only way that mankind can rule rightly *for* God. Mankind was made to rule for God in this world, but it was only ever possible with the inner resources that come from God. Left to our own devices, this world, its people as well as the rest of its animal and plant life, would, to a greater or lesser extent, suffer the effects of human misrule whether through the tyranny of oppressive regimes or the incompetence of benign ones.

The sad thing is it was never meant to be this way. We were made to rule, but just as the mandate to rule was derived from God so also, in relating and submitting to him, we were to find the mental acumen and the spiritual wisdom that were needed for the task. Again, in the words of this psalm, it was in knowing '*the* LORD' as '*our* Lord' that God intended we should rule over this world which is his by ownership and ours only for stewardship.

THE BIG ISSUE

So, relating to God, *the* LORD, as *our* Lord, was and is to be the key to finding our God-given identity (reflecting his glory) and fulfilling our God-given purpose (ruling his creation).

However, when King David took up his pen to write this psalm, these were not the thoughts uppermost in his mind; whether they are news to us or not, they were not news to him. These truths were simply part of the revelation of God and his purposes evident from the creation all around and above him. That revelation of God would have been endorsed in the instruction he would have received in his parents' home and among the wider Israelite community of which his family was a part.

No, in this psalm David is not simply repeating a creed; still less is he creating one. Rather, he is marvelling at what he believes. The twin truths of God as creator, and of man made in God's image to rule for him in his world, can be considered separately in our minds. But now the writer puts them together and alongside each other they blow the human mind. Reading the psalm with care, perhaps out loud, reveals the writer's sense of wonder and amazement. Clearly King David was no absent-minded dreamer; he was a busy man with a multitude of pressing and practical tasks which kept his feet firmly on the ground. But one night he stops to *consider* the vastness of the universe around him in comparison with the littleness of himself, and his fellow human beings:

> [3]When I consider your heavens, the work of your fingers,
> the moon and the stars, which you have set in place,
> [4]what is man that you are mindful of him,
> the son of man that you care for him? (Ps. 8:3-4).

There are only two responses one can make when we consider thoughtfully the disparity between the majesty of the universe and the microscopic nature of humankind inhabiting planet Earth. The first is to conclude that we are indeed as insignificant as we are small; just specks of dust, on a minor planet, in an unimportant galaxy. Reputedly, Franklin D. Roosevelt used to have a little ritual with the famous naturalist, William Beebe. After an evening's chat the two men would go outside and look into the night sky. Gazing into the stars, they would find the lower, left-hand corner of the great square of Pegasus. One of them would recite these words, as part of their ritual: 'That is a spiral galaxy of Andromeda. It is as large as our Milky Way. It is one of a hundred million

21

galaxies. It is 750,000 light years away. It consists of 100 billion suns, each larger than our sun.' Then they would pause, and Roosevelt would finally say, 'Now I think we feel small enough. Let us go to bed!'[5]

The other response is to conclude that although we are microscopically small in comparison with the vast universe we inhabit, nevertheless God has assigned to us, of all creatures anywhere, a position of real prominence and a status of real significance – called to care for his world. And further, that we are loved and cared for by him.

The psalm writer is committed by his own observation to this second response. It is self-evident to him that the creator has assigned to mankind the unique function of ruling over his world, so we are not simply insignificant specks of dust or just clever monkeys. The breathtaking thought for King David is that the mighty and majestic God, whose glory is everywhere evident to him in creation, does indeed care for little you and little me. To King David it is wonderful that it should be so.

It is worth a momentary detour to ask where else men and women find any sense of dignity and significance. The plain and awful truth is that many find none and, for some, suicide is an obvious way to end the vain, painful and meaningless charade that is life. The year I consciously became a Christian believer, 1977, was also the year that more people than ever before jumped to their death from the Golden Gate Bridge, San Francisco.

Others with a more sanguine disposition are not so pessimistic. Life may indeed be without ultimate purpose or meaning but in the absence of any authorised version of what a human life should be like, or the purpose it should fulfil, the world is a luxury man-made playground.

---

5   Quoted in *How to Find God* by David C.K. Watson. According to more recent figures, Andromeda is approximately 2.5 million light years away and has 10^{12} stars.

There is music and sport, art and drama, money and sex, family and friends, qualifications and careers. And these activities and pleasures amply provide a sense of dignity, significance and worth. The work that I do, the possessions I accumulate and the relationships I enjoy provide me with all the satisfaction I seek.

But if there is no creator God, life *is* meaningless. Work and recreation, friends and family, money and possessions may dull the pain, and will increase the pleasure, but they cannot provide a purpose or attach value or worth to our lives in an objective and ultimate sense. It's a thought that many have expressed in music and song:

> I suppose that you think you matter.
> Well how much do you matter to whom?
> It's much easier at night, when with friends and bright
>   lights
> Than much later alone in your room.
>
> Do you think they'll miss one in a billion
> When you finish this old human race?
> Does it really make much of a difference
> When friends have forgotten your face?[6]

The autobiographical *A Child Called 'It'* by Dave Pelzer is just one book which develops this theme of the worth of a human being. As a child the author was brutally beaten and starved by his emotionally unstable, alcoholic mother; a mother who played tortuous, unpredictable games that left one of her sons nearly dead. She no longer considered him a son, but a slave; no longer a boy, but an 'it'.

Is that just a one-off 'bad luck' story? What if we could go to a rubbish tip in a poor part of the world and find there an abandoned and deformed baby, and ask the

---

6   Selected stanzas extracted from a song by Graham Kendrick (1974).

question: does that baby have value and worth? What answer would conventional human wisdom, operating outside of a framework of faith in a creator God, give to that question? If there is no God and no-one ascribing value to that abandoned baby then presumably the child has no value. A person may respond that if they were passing by that rubbish tip, they would rescue and care for the child – thus giving him or her a value. It is true that in those circumstances the child is of value to the person providing the care. But the question remains – does the baby have a value in circumstances where no such person passes by; does the baby have intrinsic value? And the answer that King David would give is 'yes'. That child, whether cared for by anyone or not, has been made by God in God's image and likeness.

The point of this argument, taken to extremes, is simply to highlight that either we are worthless, as the atheistic philosophies of our world must ultimately tell us (if they are honest), or else we do have a real value. The writer of the psalm is saying we have a value which is not dependent on our achievements, possessions and relationships, and varying with these 'signs of worth'. Our real worth is fixed, not floating, and a matter of sober certainty, not wishful thinking. It is grounded in the fact that we are made by God and are infinitely valuable to him. And again it is wonderful to our writer that this is so.

Therefore this psalm teaches us where to go in search of an answer to the question, 'Am I worth anything?' We should not go to our possessions; they may be gone tomorrow, and one day quite soon we leave them all behind. We should not look to our achievements; they are surely much less significant than we fondly and vainly imagine, and if we could peer into the future we should find the history books remember us little and credit us with less. 'There is no remembrance of men of old, and even those who are yet to come will not be remembered by those who follow.'[7] We should not ask our friends; they may flatter us, knowing that our fragile egos could not bear too much truth. 'Even people who swear to remember you are not really going to do so.'[8] We must go to the eternal God.

God alone, our perfectly good creator, and absolutely just judge, sees everything and knows us completely. Therefore, God alone is in a perfect position to give the true assessment worth hearing and heeding, namely that we are immensely valuable, for he made us and cares for us.

The question remains whether we can see God for who he is, and trust him for the value he places on our lives.

BLAND OR BLIND?

What makes the author of this psalm rather different from most of us is that he sees God clearly. Today a few are vocal in their antipathy to the god they do not believe in. More are living with a veiled hostility to God. But for so many, the God of our writer here is not present to their consciousness. He evokes no great paeans of praise or violent expressions of defiant opposition. God, if he exists, is bland. Perhaps an experience of church confirms a suspicion that few believe in a God who fills the horizons of the mind of man in the way that he fills the horizons for the writer of this psalm: 'O LORD, our Lord, how majestic is your name in all the earth! You have set your glory above the heavens' (Ps. 8:1).

---

7 A quotation from the book of Ecclesiastes (1:11), which explores with candour the meaninglessness of a life without God.

8 Celebrated atheist, Christopher Hitchens, in the final stages of cancer, talking to Mick Brown, in *The Telegraph,* March 2011.

But what Christians believe, however poorly they may make it known, is that God is magnificent! And if we do not see that, it is not because God is bland but because we are blind and need the eyes of our minds to be opened. The story is told of a man at Speakers' Corner speaking scornfully on one occasion, 'They tell me there is a God; but I don't see him! They tell me there is a heaven; but I don't see it! They tell me there is a hell; but I don't see that!' There was a great deal of approval and applause for these common and popular sentiments. After a while, a second speaker rose to the platform. 'They tell me…', he began falteringly, '…they tell me there is green grass, but I've never seen it. They tell me there is a blue sky, but I've never seen that. They tell me there are crowds of people all around me, but I've never seen them. You see, I'm blind.'

Spiritually, this is the human condition. We need to be able to pray a prayer along the lines of: 'God, if you are there, and if you are the majestic and glorious God of which the writer of this psalm here speaks and sings, open my eyes, and cause me to see.' And if God were to open our eyes to see what the writer here sees, what would fill our minds and hearts? We would see the one God, combining in his one self both the awesome creative power that has brought everything into existence and a real care towards the people he has made, little you and little me.[9] Jesus spoke of this God, when he taught his disciples to pray 'Our Father, who art in Heaven'. To speak of God as 'in heaven' is to speak of his limitless power: 'Our God is in heaven; he does whatever pleases him' (Ps. 115:3). To speak of God as Father is to speak of his personal care for his children. So Jesus can say '… do not worry, saying, "What shall we eat?" or "What shall we drink?" or

---

9   The major objection to this in people's minds is the fact of human suffering. See 'Jill asks' at the close of this chapter.

26

"What shall we wear?" For the pagans run after all these things, and your heavenly Father knows that you need them.'(Matt. 6:31-32) The amazing truth of this psalm is that you and I can know, and be cared for by, the all-powerful and utterly personal creator God of the universe.

KNOWING GOD

In this vision of God, majestic in power and mindful of mankind made in his image, lies the solid and wonderful assurance that our lives have a value and living has a purpose.

From this vantage point it is clear that the important questions to ask and answer are the questions about how we may know this God personally. In this psalm King David starts to address that question for he recognises that there is a right and a wrong way of relating to God. And already in the present, mankind divides in its response to God. We shall either submit to God or scoff at him:

> From the lips of children and infants you have ordained praise because of your enemies, to silence the foe and the avenger (Ps. 8:2).

Faced with the enormous claims that are made for God in this psalm, it is inevitable that we shall either acknowledge him as our God, or we shall reject him.

Certainly God has enemies; indeed it is characteristic of human nature to live as God's enemies.[10] But, equally, God is at work in his world to raise up a choir and chorus of praise to him as the majestic and glorious creator God. And very often an ability to see God for who he is comes from unlikely places. In this psalm it is not the wise and learned among men who see God for who he is and submit to him. It is 'children and infants'

---

10   See chapter 5.

who see God for who he is and whom God chooses to bear witness to him with praise and adoration.

But what exactly is involved in acknowledging the LORD as our Lord? Must we simply sing songs morning, noon and night? Is heaven simply playing harps on a celestial cloud? Does God really need the endless adoration that he seems bent on procuring?[11]

The answer, as we have begun to see, is not that God needs the praise that we can bestow, but that we need the God that has created us, if we are to fulfil our human potential according to his divine plan. Relating rightly to God is the key both to reflecting his glory in our lives, and ruling in this world for him.

Here in this psalm it is clear that relating rightly to God is not the function of our lips alone. Certainly a life which rightly relates to God will include the praise of lips that confess his name, and that exalt him in music and song; this psalm is one such song of praise to God: 'O LORD, our Lord, how majestic is your name in all the earth!' But relating rightly to God is about more than the songs we sing. Praise that is worthy of God needs to be expressed not only by the words and songs of our lips, but also – and crucially – by the direction and devotion of our lives. 'The children and infants' who here praise God, are contrasted with the 'foe and the avenger' who are God's enemies and who oppose him; singing Christmas carols each year is no sign of – or substitute for – a God-centred life.

THANK YOU, BUT NO THANK YOU.

But what will determine whether I will be among those who see God for who he is, and come to know him

---

11   'Why does God want us to glorify him? Is he needy?' This is a commonly asked and keenly felt question. See 'Jack asks' at the close of this chapter.

personally as my God, or whether I will be among those who neither see him nor know him? One part of the answer is found by asking a further question, namely 'do I *want* to see and know God?'

If our spiritual couldn't-care-less-ness is really our blindness rather than God's blandness, we will be helped by learning not to be so easily satisfied with such small things and little pleasures that commonly keep us content! We were made for such great joys and such lasting treasures!

Perhaps we have seen children squabbling over a small broken toy; for them life is all about winning the fight for the toy! Perhaps we are intrigued and enraptured by the boyfriend or girlfriend, husband or wife, family or friends. Life, we think, can get no better than being with them! Or maybe we are satisfied by the social esteem and financial security that accompanies success in our career. Once we have this, we have arrived!

And yet all the time, the majestic God of the universe beckons us to enjoy the 'eternal pleasures at his right hand'(Ps. 16:11) of which the delights offered by possessions, relationships and success in this world are just a very faint echo and a most dim reflection. We may answer 'thank you, but no thank you' to the offer of knowing our creator God. But if the psalmist is right – and I say 'no thank you to God' – I lose out on the purpose for which I was made – the knowledge of God, majestic in his power and intimate in his care.

Our writer makes no such mistake in this psalm. His mind is filled with his vision of God's majesty. His horizons are filled with a picture of God's glory. His heart is humbled by the thought of God's power. His lips are full of God's praise. His life is a considered reflection on the theme of God's care for his creation, and mankind as the pinnacle of the created order. His life truly presents a well-ordered existence, in the centre of which is the Creator God highly and rightly esteemed.

BIG QUESTIONS

JACK ASKS:
You say that God is the creator. Does that mean Christians believe evolution is all wrong; that the universe was created in six days and that Homo sapiens is about 6,000 years old?

JONATHAN ANSWERS:
Not necessarily. For all the clashes there have been historically between science and religion, they are essentially asking and answering two entirely different questions. The scientific method (and many Christians are scientists and committed to that) is addressing the question '*how*' – for example '*how* has this world come to take its present form?', or '*how* have human beings come into existence?' Christianity, however, is essentially asking the question '*why?*' or '*who?*' – for example '*why* are we here?' or '*who* brought us into existence?'

Where scientists can explain *how* something has come to pass, they have not explained God away, although some of us with a non-scientific background may mistakenly interpret their findings in that way. Rather, they have explained how God has been at work in the exercise of his creative powers. This perspective on the fruits of scientific research has been spoken of as 'thinking God's thoughts after him'[12] – as we are able to give a scientific explanation

---

12 The German astronomer, Johannes Kepler, is credited with saying that through his study of the universe he was 'thinking God's thoughts after him'.

for a particular phenomenon we observe, and which we are able to continue to attribute ultimately to God's divine power and creative initiative. To use an analogy, someone might observe that the kettle is boiling, and by way of explanation say that the heat of the element applied to the water causes a transfer of energy to the water molecules so that they move around vigorously, with some escaping into the atmosphere causing steam to be given off. An alternative explanation for a boiling kettle might be that Dad has put the kettle on so we can have a cup of tea. Both explanations of the boiling kettle are true but from the different perspectives of 'how' and 'why'.

So, Christians are not obliged to inhabit two contradictory thought worlds, worshipping God on a Sunday and science for the duration of the working and thinking week. I regularly say to people 'anything that a scientist can certainly tell you is certainly true', and if we Christians have read the Bible as though it were a scientific textbook (which it is not) we need to own up, come clean and say we have got it wrong. Having said all that, scientific theory concerning the origins of the universe and of the species is often just that – theory. And certainly Christians believing in a creator God, able to direct and overrule all that takes place in this world (see ch. 2) are not bound to require the very long periods of time (billions of years) required by those for whom the only possible way human beings could have arrived at their present state is by an entirely random process of accidental genetic mutation, unguided by any divine being.

But importantly, God does not contradict himself by saying one thing in Scripture and another thing in the physical and material universe of which we are a part.

It remains the case that whatever can be deduced with certainty from our creation by the scientific community is certainly true. And to acknowledge a creator God does not close down any discussion about *how* God made the world or even the timescale for that creative activity – an issue on which Christians themselves do differ in their views. To acknowledge a creator God is simply to acknowledge that, by whatever means, and over whatever period, God brought the universe into being. Equally, acknowledging God as the Creator was not a temporary explanation by and for primitive man until the process of scientific research gradually caused our world to yield up the secrets of its beginnings. If we simply use 'God' to fill the gaps of our human knowledge, then of course as human knowledge increases and the gaps in our knowledge decrease, belief in such a God ('the god of the gaps') is increasingly dispensable. But in fact whatever answers the scientific method can give as to 'how' we came to be here, these will not dispense with the question of whether there is an ultimate reason or cause ('a first cause') behind it all, addressing the question *why* we are here.

JILL ASKS:

You speak of God's limitless power and his personal care. But how can you square belief in a God that is all-powerful and loving with all the suffering in our world?

JONATHAN ANSWERS:

This objection to the God in whom Christians believe resonates with all thinking, feeling people. For example, when a newspaper headline reads: 'The hidden massacre', and the report continues, 'more than 20,000 Tamil civilians were killed in the final throes of the Sri Lankan civil war, most as a result of government shelling...', we are bound to ask where is a God of power and love in that situation?

It is worth considering the alternative viewpoint for a moment. If the fact of suffering (of which you may have personal, painful experience) does indeed make belief in a powerful and loving God impossible or incredible, two consequences follow. First, we remain (as indeed with those who believe differently) locked up in a world where there is bound to be tremendous suffering; our 'unbelief' will not, of course, change the raw data of human experience. But second – and this will be different – we are locked up in a world view that can offer no meaning in life, no comfort in suffering and no prospect of light at the end of the tunnel – only death and with it (hopefully) destruction of the sensation of pain. Arguably this world view multiplies our suffering; at the very least it does nothing to make the pain more bearable. Most likely it makes the alleviation of pain and the pursuit of pleasure primary goals of our existence (albeit ultimately fruitless ones).

But is there an alternative? Can we square the existence of a God of love and power with what we experience of suffering in our world? There is no one clear and definitive answer to the problem of pain and suffering. But the Bible does give some indications of why it is that the fact of pain and suffering is not necessarily at odds with the existence of a God of love and power.

First, God in his love has given us freedom to make choices. A human parent *could* protect a child from a great deal of suffering by taking away a great deal of freedom. If the child is to be free to ride a bicycle, the child will sooner or later experience the pain of a fall. The bruises and bleeding that may follow should not be interpreted as a lack of parental love. Unless God were perpetually to suspend the natural laws of cause and effect – which would indeed make this universe totally unpredictable and truly treacherous – the thrill of riding a bike will involve the risk of a crash and the thrill of climbing a mountain will involve the risk of a fall; being humans, with bodies, will involve physical suffering.

But, secondly, what are we to make of 'natural disasters'? What human choices are made there? It is true that for all that this world is in many ways safely sustaining the lives of seven billion or so people, it is not an absolutely safe and human-friendly environment. There are floods and droughts, tsunamis and hurricanes. They wreak a terrible havoc. We need to know the Bible doesn't ignore this. And indeed it doesn't. On the contrary, it is explicit in teaching that one consequence of the human race turning from God (more of this in subsequent chapters) is that the physical environment we occupy is corrupted too.[13] It is no longer the perfectly good creation God made it to be. It is broken. A great deal of suffering occurs when human neglect of our role as stewards of this creation fails to reckon with the fact of the broken world we inhabit.

For example, the earthquake that struck Haiti on 13th January 2010 reputedly claimed the lives of 200,000 people. 'There's the all-powerful, all-loving God you talk about,' someone might comment cynically. But as one journalist commented, 'This was a man-made disaster.' 'This is not a natural disaster story,' said David Brooks in *The New York Times*. 'This is a poverty story. In October 1989,

---

13   God says to disobedient Adam, *'Cursed is the ground because of you...'* (Gen. 3:17). And the apostle Paul, speaking of the redemption of humanity preceding the renewal of creation, says, *'The creation waits in eager expectation for the sons of God to be revealed. For the creation was subjected to frustration, not by its own choice, but by the will of the one who subjected it, in hope that the creation itself will be liberated from its bondage to decay and brought into the glorious freedom of the children of God'* (Rom. 8:19-21).

another quake of magnitude 7.0 hit the densely populated but wealthy Bay Area in Northern California; only sixty-three people died.' 'The toll in Haiti was both predictable and avoidable,' agreed David Rothkopf in *Newsweek*. 'The world's "mega-disasters" – 2008's earthquake in Sichuan, China; cyclone Hargis in Burma; the Indian Ocean tsunami – almost always follow a pattern. Vulnerable communities set up home on 'treacherous soil: below sea level, on mountains, or along fault lines. Weak or incompetent governments fail to establish building codes, early-warning systems, rescue protocols or protective infrastructure such as sea walls – and nature does the rest.'[14]

Thirdly, God's love is, once again, not incompatible with suffering in circumstances where God, in his love, has actively warned us not to pursue a way of life that will lead to suffering. A loving human parent warns a child if the child's actions will lead to suffering. And in a similar way God speaks to warn us when our life's trajectory leads away from him – which essentially is what hell (the ultimate suffering) would be: separation from God and from the presence of everything good that God has made.

Finally, God in his love has worked to undo the effects of suffering. It is sickness and death that strike us as the most unjust and undeserved of suffering. How is this suffering compatible with a God of love? The short answer is that disease and death are no part of God's original design for mankind; they are themselves 'unnatural' intruders into our human existence. Nevertheless, they are among the consequences that God predicted would follow from human rebellion against him. In a general sense we may say suffering and death are the deserved consequences of the whole of mankind's rebellion against God. But the good news of God's love

---

14 *The Week* news journal 23rd January 2010.

spoken of in the Bible is that suffering and death need not be the end for anyone. At great cost to himself God has made a way whereby we might be rescued ultimately from these intruders into the perfectly good world that God originally made. Later chapters will explore this.

Perhaps this question is asked by someone who is presently suffering greatly. You should take comfort that Jesus, in his teaching, explicitly warns against trying to find the particular cause of individual suffering in a person's particular sin[15] – as though all suffering were a present-day judgment of God. Rather, all suffering can, in God's economy, both alert us to the dangers we face without him, and also point us to him as the one who can rescue us from the ultimate suffering of being God-forsaken.[16]

JACK ASKS:
Why does God command us to worship him? It sounds as though he is needy in some way, or 'self centred'!

JONATHAN ANSWERS:
This, too, is a commonly stated objection to what Christians believe. The answer is not that God is 'needy' of what we can supply to him, but that we are needful of what he supplies to us.

He needs nothing we can supply – something we will explore further in the following chapter. Nonetheless, when Jesus is asked which is the greatest commandment in the Law, he replies, '"Love the Lord your God with all your heart and with all your soul and with all your mind." This is the first and greatest

---

15 John 9:1-3.
16 Luke 13:1-5.

commandment.'(Matt. 22:37-38, where Jesus quotes Deut. 6:5). To put it another way, God has made us to worship him. Why so?

The essential answer is that God has made us in such a way that we reach our human potential when we acknowledge our creaturely status rather than try to play God. This is because he alone is worthy of the praise and adoration of our lips and lives. And if our lives are not, first of all, an expression of love for God and a declaration of *his* greatness, then we live to glorify something or someone that is not worth the ultimate adoration of our hearts – in other words, we live a lie and we are less than human as a result. That someone or something may be myself, or a husband, wife or child, or pleasure, work or wealth. But whoever or whatever it may be, Jesus is saying nothing and no-one has a higher claim on the love and loyalty of our lives than God alone.

Beyond that, as we have begun to see in this last chapter, to worship God, as he commands, will not impoverish us – rather, it will enrich us. For without relating rightly to God, giving him the supreme place in our affections, and honouring him as the rightful ruler of our lives, we are not able to fulfil the purposes for which he has made us: the purposes of reflecting his image and glory and ruling for him in this world.

Finally, God calls us to honour and worship him because this, and this alone, is the way of joy and happiness and – yes – God created us for *our* joy as well as *his*. So it proves to be the case that our duty (to love God with everything we are) is both our duty and our delight. As one of the church's catechisms puts it, we are made by God 'to glorify God and to enjoy him forever'. And, as others have pointed out, these are not two separate aims but one: we glorify God in the very business of enjoying him and delighting in him.

****

One way of clarifying *what Christians believe* is – positively – to state it, as we have begun to do in this chapter. Another way of clarifying that same faith is to identify some ways in which it is effectively misunderstood – and that is the different approach of the next chapter.

However much we may admire and appreciate the 'positive' process of identifying and affirming what Christians *do* believe, we will be helped in our understanding by clarifying what Christians do not believe and by exposing common errors which confuse and deceive us.

Many of us only half believe 'what Christians believe' because we have believed things that Christians do *not* believe. Having these errors exposed – ideas that are often comfortable to us and cherished by us – can be rather painful. But, as we shall see in the following chapter, believing certain truths does involve forsaking certain errors.

2 Common mistakes

When the Christian message meets a person, that individual is already a person with convictions. In the course of life, views have been shaped and convictions developed. Those views may be held firmly or more tentatively, they may be specific or fairly general, and they may be held consciously or unconsciously. But none of us has a clean slate inside our minds on which the Christian message may be written. On the contrary, there is a great deal that has been written there by all kinds of experiences we have had, and all kinds of teaching and thinking to which we have been exposed.

When we first hear the Christian message, there is, therefore, a battle for the mind – a battle being fought by competing and conflicting views of reality. On the one side there will be the accumulated convictions of all the years we have lived, and on the other will stand the newly presented truths of the Christian faith. So also, unless a reader of these pages has already accepted the Christian message before reading them, by the end there will be this same battle for the mind.

TRUE OR FALSE?

The first challenge for me listening to the Christian message, therefore, is likely to be a challenge not to the way I live but to the way I think – though the two will certainly be closely connected. And that battle for my mind is unlikely to be resolved without some difficulty. If I am to believe what Christians believe, I shall need convincing that much about which I have been ignorant or dismissive is actually true, and that some of my sincerely held convictions have been mistaken.

We may say instinctively, if not explicitly, to someone who tells us with real conviction what Christians believe, 'How arrogant you are. You think you know everything. What makes you think you are right and I am wrong?' Or we may not. We may think, 'I accept your right to believe what you do, and you should have the humility to accept what I say and believe to be true too.'

There is no doubt this second position looks more gracious and less dismissive. In the end, however, it is illogical to suppose that two contradictory propositions can *both* be right. It may look humble to believe one set of truths concerning the nature of God and the purpose of our creation, whilst simultaneously affirming other people in their own contradictory sets of ideas and beliefs, but it is not honest. If $2+2$ does equal 4, and I believe $2+2$ equals 5, someone will need the courage of their convictions, and some love for me, to tell me I am wrong. That courage is demonstrated in one of the early Christian sermons recorded in the book of Acts (otherwise known as Acts of the Apostles – a history of the early years of the church, and its first leaders).

In one such sermon the speaker is the early Christian leader or 'apostle' – the word means 'one who is sent' – Paul. He is not only explaining central and fundamental convictions about the Christian faith, he is also refuting the false ideas that his hearers have mistakenly believed. Proclaiming the truth of the Christian faith must also involve refuting error; not everything that has been written on the sheet of a person's life can be affirmed as true when the message of the Christian faith is explained. Some things will be shown up for the errors they are. And that, as we shall see, is good news.

It may surprise us to see that the mistakes and ideas in first-century Athens are common mistakes in the world of religious belief in our twenty-first century, and in reflecting on this speech we may hear our own cherished notions of reality weighed and found wanting:

[16]While Paul was waiting for Silas and Timothy in Athens, he was greatly distressed to see that the city was full of idols. [17]So he reasoned in the synagogue with the Jews and God-fearing Greeks, as well as in the market place day by day with those who happened to be there. [18]A group of Epicurean and Stoic philosophers began to dispute with him. Some of them asked, 'What is this babbler trying to say?' Others remarked, 'He seems to be advocating foreign gods.' They said this because Paul was preaching the good news about Jesus and the resurrection. [19]Then they took him and brought him to a meeting of the Areopagus, where they said to him, 'May we know what this new teaching is that you are presenting? [20]You are bringing some strange ideas to our ears, and we want to know what they mean.' [21](All the Athenians and the foreigners who lived there spent their time doing nothing but talking about and listening to the latest ideas.)

[22]Paul then stood up in the meeting of the Areopagus and said: 'Men of Athens! I see that in every way you are very religious. [23]For as I walked around and looked carefully at your objects of worship, I even found an altar with this inscription: TO AN UNKNOWN GOD.

Now what you worship as something unknown I am going to proclaim to you.

[24]'The God who made the world and everything in it is the Lord of heaven and earth and does not live in temples built by hands. [25]And he is not served by human hands, as if he needed anything, because he himself gives all men life and breath and everything else. [26]From one man he made every nation of men, that they should inhabit the whole earth; and he determined the times set for them and the exact places where they should live. [27]God did this so that men would seek him and perhaps reach out for him and find him, though he is not far from each one of us. [28]'For in him we live and move and have our being". As some of your own poets have said, "We are his offspring".

[29]'Therefore since we are God's offspring, we should not think that the divine being is like gold or silver or stone – an image made by man's design and skill. [30]In the past God overlooked such ignorance, but now he commands all people everywhere to repent. [31]For he has set a day when he will judge the world with justice by the man he has appointed. He has given proof of this to all men by raising him from the dead'.

[32]When they heard about the resurrection of the dead, some of them sneered, but others said, 'We want to hear you again on this subject'. [33]At that, Paul left the Council. [34]A few men became followers of Paul and believed. Among them was Dionysius, a member of the Areopagus, also a woman named Damaris, and a number of others. (Acts 17:16-34)

THE ARROGANCE OF THE MISSIONARY

In matters of religion, many assume there is no such thing as right and wrong, but that there are simply many different ways of seeing and describing the same fundamental truths. On this view the religions of the world are just so many different, but equally valid, paths up the mountain that leads to God.

But Paul here did not think this was so; for him, a city full of idols was not impressive, it was distressing. He was not mentally reaching for his camera to record this tremendous display of human creativity; he was mentally reaching for a sledgehammer to cast it down. For even to the people of the great city of Athens, all these objects of worship did not reflect any real certainty they had found the truth. On the contrary, these idols left them painfully exposed to the potential pitfall of not having given due honour to a god they did not know.

And to cover themselves against the possibility of giving offence to an unacknowledged but powerful god, they even had an altar with this inscription: 'TO AN UNKNOWN GOD'. Religion can operate in the same sort of way today; less an expression of conviction, and more a kind of insurance policy against the possibility of upsetting God if, in the end, it turns out that he does exist.

But is it possible to be sure of what is true? Paul says, 'Now what you worship as something unknown I am going to proclaim to you'. How could he presume to do that? Here is the 'arrogance of the missionary' people talk about, the person who 'imposes his views on people who happen to believe different things'.

How could this preacher, Paul, presume to know what these people did not know – the truth about God? There are three alternative explanations for Paul's breathtaking self-confidence. One is that these 'dear people in Athens', for all their learning and religious instinct, were actually rather primitive people without the benefit of a good education and much intelligence. But that does not fit. Here are sophisticated and intelligent philosophers in the intellectual capital of the world at that time, with every opportunity to hear and discuss the latest ideas, which this passage, as other history, tells us was indeed their occupation.

There is no suggestion Paul is belittling their intelligence, or pouring scorn on their knowledge, and no hint that he is setting himself up as their intellectual superior. If that were so, he might convince them he knew a thing or two, but he would only leave them vulnerable to the next itinerant preacher, cleverer than he, and with a different religious insight, taking them back to square one.

A second alternative is that Paul has had an altogether extraordinary religious experience, and he just had to tell everyone about it. On this view the preacher Paul was just another religious fanatic who sought to make his own religious experience the yardstick by which every religious claim was to be measured and authenticated. But again, this does not fit the facts. It is, of course, true that Paul has had a remarkable experience,[1] but he makes nothing of it here – indeed he doesn't even mention it. Besides, what does one man's experience on its own prove? History is littered with examples of men and women who have had all kinds of religious experiences.

REASON OR REVELATION?
There is a third alternative which is that the preacher Paul, far from having greater powers of reasoning than others, or indeed more powerful religious experiences than others, is simply one of that nation of people to whom the creator God of this world has revealed himself. Paul, in common with the Jewish people of his day, believed that God, who had made the world, had revealed himself to them:

> [1]In the past God spoke to our forefathers through the prophets at many times and in various ways, [2]but in these last days he has spoken to us by his Son, whom

---

1   See Acts of the Apostles, chapter 9.

he appointed heir of all things, and through whom he
made the universe. (Heb. 1:1-2)

The Bible is saying that knowing God is possible, not
because of our power to reason out the truth about him, but
because of the initiative God has taken to reveal the truth
about himself to us. He has revealed himself generally – to
everyone – through his creation, as we saw earlier. But he
has revealed himself specifically – to the nation of Israel –
through the patriarchs and prophets: 'In the past God spoke
to our forefathers through the prophets at many times and
in various ways...' And not only so, but says this writer, 'in
these last days [God] has spoken to us by his Son...'.

The idea that God has taken the initiative in revealing
himself to the people of this world is a wonderful
thought with a remarkable consequence: it means that
we need not be in the dark about what God is like, or
about what he requires of us.

More common today than atheism, the belief that there
is *no* god, is 'agnosticism', the belief that we cannot *know*
whether there is a god. It was a word coined by Thomas
Huxley at a meeting of the Metaphysical Society in 1876.
For Huxley, agnosticism was a position which rejected the
knowledge claims of both 'strong' atheism and traditional
theism. But the Bible is not sympathetic to those who
say, with Huxley, 'I cannot know'. For the Bible's human
authors are saying that God has not left us to ourselves to
flounder in a sea of unknowing, but that he has actually
taken the initiative to reveal himself to us.

The Bible is saying God has done this in two ways.
First, he has revealed himself through what he has done.
He has made our universe, and the universe reveals him
as its maker; the existence and power of the creator is
revealed by his creation. This is a revelation God makes
to all the people of this world.

And then, secondly, God has revealed himself by what he has said: God has spoken. The Jewish nation of Jesus' day was the custodian of God's self-revelation through his spoken Word. 'In the past God *spoke* to our forefathers through the prophets at many times and in various ways'. Therefore for a Jew of Jesus' day to have said 'I cannot know whether there is a God' would not have been a humble agnosticism but a proud rejection of God's revelation of himself. If God reveals himself, as the Bible says he has, through deed and word, through what he has made and what he has said, humility on our part doesn't reject his revelation; it receives it.

So when Paul comes to Athens, he is not pitting his brain against theirs, or his religious experience against theirs. He is simply saying to these clever and religiously minded people, this is what God has revealed to us. Therefore, I can tell you what you say you do not know, and indeed what cannot be known with certainty without God's initiative in speaking to his people. And it is not arrogance on the part of those who have received God's revelation of himself to pass it on with confidence. On the contrary, *not* to listen to God, *not* to believe him, *not* to pass on the record of his words and deeds to others – *that* is arrogant, because it sets us up as greater authorities than God himself. We may do it – as we think – nicely, kindly, thoughtfully, gently and reasonably, but a refusal to take God at his word is not humble.

But the preacher Paul's confidence in front of the Athenian philosophers should be seen as a sign of his humility, as Paul faithfully passed on what had been entrusted to him and his people. And yet, for all that Paul was simply a messenger of God's revelation, we cannot help observing his courage. He now addresses some of the mistakes commonly made by the religious, as illustrated in the lives of the people of Athens, and he begins to refute them one by one. See how the word '*not*' occurs time and time again as Paul defines the truth about God.

GOD...DOES *NOT* LIVE IN TEMPLES BUILT BY HUMAN HANDS

A first mistake that Paul identifies among the people of Athens is seeking to confine the creator to *a part* of his creation.

Religious people tend to deny the existence of a creator God not by denying his existence wholescale, but by imagining that any such creator can be locked up in a building, such as a temple or a church. This thinking betrays itself in all attempts to define coming to church or temple as coming to be with God in a way that is not possible elsewhere. Certainly Christians place a high value on meeting together with God's people, but if we need to be in a particular place to meet with God, then the Almighty Creator has been tamed and contained. But, says Paul, 'The God who made the world and everything in it is the Lord of heaven and earth and does *not* live in temples built by hands'.[2] The creator cannot be confined to any part of his creation.

On the floor of St Paul's Cathedral, under the dome, there is an epitaph to Sir Christopher Wren, the man who in his lifetime built that vast and majestic cathedral. The epitaph, written in Latin, is usually translated 'Reader, if you seek his memorial – look around you.' In a similar way, if we seek a monument to God that speaks of him, we need to 'look around us' – not to any

---

2   It is true that God himself instructed King Solomon to build a temple along the lines of a design given to his father King David. But Solomon knew full well that God could not be confined to that place. In his prayer of dedication of the newly built temple, Solomon prays 'But will God really dwell on earth with men? The heavens, even the highest heavens, cannot contain you. How much less this temple that I have built!' (2 Chron. 6:18).

church or temple built by hands – but to our world, our universe and everything in it that he has made.

And if I want to meet with the creator God, I will not find him in a man-made building, but I will catch a glimpse of him as I survey the creation he has made. On a holiday in the Swiss Alps, I recall a chaplain inviting the congregation to meditate on God in the silence of the chapel. But I can't have been alone in thinking that the magnificent vistas of the Alps and the north face of the Eiger gave a much clearer view of God's majesty than the inside of a homely chapel. God has created every place; he cannot be confined to any place.

But does anyone really think that God can be locked up in a building? A decline in churchgoing in England in the latter part of the twentieth century may at its best suggest that fewer people fall for this particular error. An alternative explanation is that among those who do not attend church, synagogue or temple, the belief persists that somehow religious buildings *do* contain God, with the happy consequence that if God is locked up in them he does not interfere with the rest of life, or lay claim to the lives of those who avoid these religious buildings! Of course, nothing could be further from the truth! The God who, Paul explains, 'does not live in temples built by hands' is interested not only in the lives of those who attend them. The God who 'made the world and everything [and everyone] in it' seeks to be known and honoured as the God of all those he has made. The God who does not live in temples seeks those who do not attend them.

GOD...IS *NOT* SERVED BY HUMAN HANDS
If common mistake number one is to confine God to a place, the second common mistake flows from it; it is to imagine that just as men built the place for God to

48

dwell, so man must serve and support the God who is supposed to dwell there. Once we have localised God, so he is no longer all-present, it is inevitable we shall trivialise him, so he is no longer all-powerful. He will become the God to whom we must bring food and water, the God for whom we must provide a place of shelter. From now on we shall need to look to his interests so he does not fall into disrepair or disrepute. But once again, this could not be further from the truth; there is nothing God needs you or me to do for him:

> And he is not served by human hands, as if he needed anything, because he himself gives all men life and breath and everything else. (Acts 17:25)

Most of us have not consciously tried to serve God with food or water, such as you might find the devotees doing in a Hindu temple, but it is surprisingly easy to think of relating to God in terms of something we will do for God, rather than in terms of being reliant on him for everything he has given to us – including life itself. In a measure some churches are responsible for cultivating this attitude, holding out the 'begging bowl' to the general public to fix the church roof or spire, and giving the entirely false impression that God, and God's cause, is somehow dependent on us – as if to say 'God's cause is rather needy at the moment: please give whatever you can.'

But if the churches mislead people in this way, it is a deception in which the proud human heart is only too willing to be complicit. It suits the human spirit to be able to patronise God, and God's people, with gifts (helping the local church in this way and that), when the reality is quite otherwise: but for what comes to each of us from the hand of God, we would have nothing whatever to give to him. The Christian prayer expresses this truth when it says: 'All things come from you, O Lord, and of your own have we given you' (1 Chron. 29:14). Even the breath I breathe now is only possible because the creator God sustains me in being alive at this moment. And if at any moment God were to withdraw his hand and withhold my breath, my earthly life would be at an end.

GOD...IS *NOT* FAR FROM EACH ONE OF US

There is a third common mistake – or convenient illusion– that we harbour in our hearts. It is that God has made himself inaccessible. If that were so, if God really had locked himself away out of reach, then of course there could be no obligation on me to know him or to honour him with my life. But, again, as Paul speaks of the truth concerning God, he confronts this common error:

> [26]From one man he made every nation of men that they should inhabit the whole earth; and he determined the times set for them and the exact places where they should live. [27]God did this so that men would seek him and perhaps reach out for him and find him, though he is not far from each one of us. [28]'For in him we live and move and have our being.' As some of your own poets have said, 'We are his offspring.' (Acts 17:26-28)

Here Paul takes the battle for their minds onto their own turf by quoting their own poets to them. God is not far away. He is not inaccessible. He is not beyond our reach. On the contrary, he is as close to us as the air we breathe: 'in him we live and move and have our being'. Nor is he impersonal and unknowable. On the contrary, he is as personal and knowable as anyone alive today, for God is like us: 'we are his offspring'.

Even more remarkable than the truth that God is both near to us and knowable by us is the fact that God is at work in this world to bring us to himself. So, says Paul, the God who has made everything and everyone exercises his sovereign control over this world (determining the times and places where the nations would live), and even over the specific circumstances of my individual life (when and where I live – even that I read these sentences now) *so that* we would seek God and 'perhaps reach out for him and find him...' The all-powerful creator God seeks a relationship with each of us and acts to make that a reality by making us seekers after him.

And that's the point here: God will commonly be found by those who 'seek him... and reach out for him'. So the quest to know God is never just a matter for an indifferent mind. It is a matter for the heart and will. A hope that God is far away, and unknowable, may prove to be a self-fulfilling desire. But the assurance here, as Paul speaks in Athens, is that a sincere desire to seek God and reach out for him will almost certainly be one aspect of a successful finding of the one who is *not* far away.

GOD ...IS *NOT* LIKE GOLD OR SILVER OR STONE

Perhaps the most fundamental error of all is forgetting or suppressing the truth that God is our creator, and actually imagining that we can create our own God. Here is Paul confronting this distortion of the truth:

> [29]Therefore since we are God's offspring, we should not think that the divine being is like gold or silver or stone – an image made by man's design and skill. [30]In the past God overlooked such ignorance, but now he commands all people everywhere to repent. (Acts 17:29-30)

To many of us, the idea that we could create God would be ludicrous. And perhaps few of us in the West today are tempted to create and worship our own gods in the crude form which Paul encounters in the Athens of his day. But historically God's people had fallen for this error,[3] and still today much religion takes this form. Many of us will be able to confirm the observations of one man who writes:

> I have travelled to northern India several times... Idolatry permeates every aspect of individual and cultural life. Stand almost anywhere in northern India and you can see an altar to one of Hinduism's many gods. One day I stood in a temple and watched a young priest feed, bathe and clothe an idol. I watched his colleague lie prostrate on the floor before an image of wood and gold. I was overcome by their sincerity and devotion. These inanimate images controlled every waking moment of the priests' lives, even though they had no ability to see, speak, or act in any way beneficial to their worshippers.[4]

Underlying the prevalence of idolatry is the fact that human beings are incurably religious by nature. Therefore, whenever and wherever the creator God is displaced in the minds and affections of men and women, *other* gods or idols take his place.

The form that takes will vary; in the Athens that Paul visited, that took the form of *metal* objects of worship. But it can just as easily take the form of *mental* objects of worship, as when I say 'I like to think of God like this ...' Such a *mental* construct in my mind is idolatry just as

---

3   'When the people saw that Moses was so long in coming down from the mountain, they gathered round Aaron and said, "Come, make us gods who will go before us. As for this fellow Moses who brought us up out of Egypt, we don't know what has happened to him". Aaron answered them, "Take off the gold ear-rings that your wives, your sons and your daughters are wearing, and bring them to me." So all the people took off their ear-rings and brought them to Aaron. He took what they handed him and made it into an idol cast in the shape of a calf, fashioning it with a tool. Then they said, "These are your gods, O Israel, who brought you up out of Egypt,"' (Exod. 32:1-4).

4   From *Instruments in the Redeemer's Hands* by Paul Tripp.

much as a *metal* object that I construct with my hands. What is common to both is a rejection of the true and living creator God, and the creation of a man-made idol to take his place. There is an appeal in idolatry which rests – as we think – in making the god we create a god we can control. On the assumption that *what* we make cannot control *we* who make it, our man-made idols seem to leave us free from their interference in a way in which the living and true God does not; they 'leave us alone'.

To be sure, our man-made idols can't help us much; there is a stupidity about idolatry. But the point is they can't require much of us either. They seem to leave us free to run our own lives in our own way. And that's appealing. C.S. Lewis spoke of God as a 'transcendental interferer' and of wanting 'to call my life my own.'[5]

The reality, however, is otherwise, as the account of these worshippers and their multitude of idols makes plain. The reality is that living in bondage to lies about God and God-substitutes in the form of idols creates a vicious slavery all of its own.

There are the petty idolatries consisting of all kinds of superstitions that we tend to believe and that end up controlling and constraining our lives – worrying about broken mirrors, black cats, walking under ladders, daily horoscopes and the rest! We might make light of these, because in the cold light of day they seem so absurd, but they can paralyse the lives of those who take them seriously.

Beyond these superficial superstitions, however, there are idols that catch many more of us, pressing us into their service with the ever-growing devotion of our lives. We began to see this in the last chapter. For example, the idol of money; the desire for more can drive a whole

---

5   C.S. Lewis in *Surprised by Joy.*

life. So also can the idol of sex; the rampant desire for satisfaction can skew a whole life, not to mention leave a trail of destruction in its wake. The idol of success can steal a person from their home and family; conversely, family and relationships can become an idol. And the idol of image and identity, displayed in a strong desire to conform, can chip away at character and integrity.

This is not to say that any of these things – money, sex, success at work, close relationships and family or indeed the aim to 'fit in' to society – are bad things. Worshippers of God are not destined for life confined to a monastery, away from the real world. No, but it does mean that if I don't know the true God, these gifts that come to us from his hand will invariably assume an importance in our lives they ought never to have. If we will not be worshippers of the one true God, we will become idolaters – just like those people in Athens that we think must have been so primitive with their carved idols and images.

In summary, each of these four errors is an error which buttresses unbelief in the creator God and so Paul exposes these errors.

We need to know that God does *not* live in temples. He made the world and everything in it, so he cannot be confined to one place but rather encountered in every place.

He is *not* served by human hands. He himself gives all men life and breath and everything else; we can offer him nothing he needs, rather we are dependent on everything he gives.

He is *not* far from each one of us. 'In him we live and move and have our being'. His invisibility is not to be confused with inaccessibility. On the contrary, he is at work in history, and in our today, to make us seekers after him – and finders too.

And he is *not* like gold or silver or stone – an image made by man's design and skill; 'we are his offspring', so we mustn't settle for a God who is less alive than the hearing, seeing, speaking, sentient creatures that we are and that he has made.

Why does it matter for Paul to expose the idolatries of the people of Athens? Because belonging to the true God is not just a question of adding him into the equation of a full life. Idols destroy. And therefore, in the goodness of God, these destroyers must themselves be destroyed – as Paul is here doing in Athens.

Idols destroy in one of two ways. Either they steal our hearts or they shape our minds. When they steal our hearts, they supplant God in our affections. It is not that family, money, sex, power, success or fame ever actually *claim* to be God. How could they? Rather, because of their appeal to our hearts we treat them as God in the sense that they simply take the place of God at a practical level in our lives. To a greater or lesser extent, we live for them; we worship them. They steal our hearts and direct our lives. They usurp the place that rightly belongs to God alone (for the reasons we saw in the earlier chapter). So, if I am asked for my 'religion' on a passport application form, or the like, I may write 'Christian'. But the truth may be that at the level of the life I live, I am really an atheist. We might say, more accurately, I am less a 'Christ-ian' than a 'money-ian' or a 'sex-ian' or a 'relationship-ian' or a 'work-ian', worshipping one or more of these god-substitutes, rather than God himself.

But idols can destroy in a second and more subtle way. They shape our minds. When we make idols, whether metal objects or mental constructs, we are very likely trying to represent God in some tangible way. And in the very process of representing God we misrepresent him. So our minds are shaped (wrongly), and we end up worshipping not the one true creator God, but rather a god of our own making – an idol.

In the Old Testament, God works very hard to keep his people from having their minds misshaped. In the first of the 'Ten Commandments', he says, 'You shall have no other gods before me'. And in the second of these Ten Commandments, he says, 'You shall not make an idol in the form of anything in heaven above or on the earth beneath or in the waters below' (Exod. 20:3-4). Why is that? Because our representations of God will always be misrepresentations of him. So we will be found to be worshipping something other than the creator God. This is the danger of 'religious art', whether three- dimensional objects or two-dimensional pictures.

Idolatry is hard to spot – in ourselves. Not many of us will be candid enough to admit 'our hearts have been stolen', and the true God usurped in our affections. Still fewer, that our 'minds have been warped' so that we are no longer worshipping the true God as we thought, but idols of our own vain imagining. But that is the truth which Paul here works to impress on his listeners in Athens.

This, then, is the conclusion to Paul's message to the idol-worshippers of Athens:

> [30]In the past God overlooked such ignorance, but now he commands all people everywhere to repent. [31]For he has set a day when he will judge the world with justice by the man he has appointed. He has given proof of this to all men by raising him from the dead. (Acts 17:30-31)[6]

---

6   See further, chapter 4.

Note that God's Word (through Paul) for them and for then is God's message for us and for today: '…he commands *all* people *everywhere* to repent.' What, then, is 'repentance'?

Perhaps surprisingly, if this is a word with which we feel familiar, 'repentance' is not first and foremost a challenge to my heart (and lifestyle) but to my mind (and thought processes). Paul is not saying here 'you have been bad, so repent and be good.' He is saying you have been ignorant, but now you know the truth, so repent and do away with your false notions about what God is like. Repentance, then, is in the first place simply acknowledging the truth about God, and recognizing him for who he is. The apostle Paul highlights a double reason to do so.

The first is that we have no excuse for ignorance about God's nature and character; he has revealed himself to us. And God's revelation of himself to us brings with it a responsibility to relate rightly to him.[7] The day the truth dawns and my ignorance of the truth about God my maker is dispelled is the day I should turn to him and determine from then on to acknowledge him for who he really is. I might pray 'Lord God, I have been blind to who you are. Please help me to live in the light of what I now know about you, the Lord of heaven and earth, and honour you as the creator and sustainer of this universe and of my life.'

Have I been living as though God dwelt in religious buildings, rather than being the creator of the universe? Then I need to repent – that is, change my mind. Have I been living as though in some way I sustained God and his cause, rather than God sustaining me and my life? Then I need to repent. Have I been living as though God was far away and hard to find, rather than close at hand and calling me to seek him? Then I need

---

7   Ignorance is not bliss, but knowledge is responsibility. See 'Jack asks' at the close of this chapter.

to repent. Have I been living as though God was an inanimate object and unknowable, rather than one of 'his offspring'? Then I need to repent. God commands all people everywhere to repent.

There is a second reason given here to repent, to change my mind about God, and that is the prospect of judgment. 'God has set a day when he will judge the world with justice by the man he has appointed. He has given proof of this to all men by raising him from the dead' (v. 31).

The big issue on judgment day will be 'Did I acknowledge God as God?' The lives we have lived may well provide *evidence* one way or another. But the issue that the available evidence addresses is, 'Was the God of this world, the Lord of my life?'

If the God of this world is a God of love, this reminder of judgment is not an arbitrary and frightening threat, but a kind and loving warning. Just as a parent might say to a child, 'Don't stand too near the track – there is a train coming' or 'Come away from the fire – or you will burn yourself', so too God in his infinite love warns us against a way of thinking and a way of living that will end on the wrong side of God's judgment. Both on account of the revelation of himself that God *has already given* to us, and in light of the day God has set when he *will certainly* judge the world with justice, God commands all people everywhere to repent. That means changing the way I think about God, which will lead in turn to changing the way I live for God.

We may have felt sorry and said sorry many times for wrong things we have done, or even the right things we have neglected to do. But the question here is, do I consciously acknowledge the creator God of this world as the rightful ruler of my life? There is all the difference in the world between rejecting God whilst endeavouring to live a good life (on the one hand), and acknowledging God even if I often fail to live the good life I know he would have me do (on the other).

A person in the first category is rejecting God and faces a rejection by God. If that is you, God commands you to repent.

If I am in the second category, then I still face the judgment but, as we shall see, the man God has appointed as judge is the very same man through whom God is able to show me mercy.[8]

The message from God, through Paul's message to the Athenians is this: the only right life to live, and indeed the only safe place to be, is living a life that is turned to acknowledge the true God for who he truly is. Such a life takes seriously what God has revealed of himself in creation and supremely through his Son (as we will see in the next chapter). And it takes seriously that one day God will judge the world with justice, by the man he has appointed. The question on that day will be 'Did I live my days for the God who made me for himself?'

BIG QUESTIONS

JACK ASKS:
What about those who have never heard about this God?

JONATHAN ANSWERS:
The assumption behind the question is that those who have not heard are unfairly, perhaps eternally, disadvantaged. Note, however, the claim here that God will judge the world with 'justice' (Acts 17:31).

---

8   This is developed further in chapters 5 and 6.

While the Bible is relatively silent about those who have never heard (including children who die in infancy, or people who are mentally incapacitated in some way), it is very clear that those who are privileged to hear clearly about God are responsible for how they respond to him.

The answer to someone who asks 'What about others?' is, in part at least, 'Leave others to the God who is perfectly just. What about you?' The knowledge that I have about God imposes a responsibility I have to honour him as my God: knowledge brings responsibility.

Having said all that, ignorance is not bliss. It is true that of Judas Iscariot (who betrayed Jesus) Jesus said, 'it would be better for him if he had not been born' (Mark 14:21). That shows that Judas' unique opportunity and his determined rejection of Jesus put him – as Jesus says – in a worse position than if he had known nothing ('not been born'). But the Bible does not generalise from this unique case and encourage us to think that the opportunity to know God is a burdensome responsibility. On the contrary, it tells us that knowledge is opportunity – opportunity to know God and his purposes for our lives (as subsequent chapters will explore).

JILL SAYS:

You say that those who seek God will find him. Well, I've been looking all my life – and I haven't found him.

JONATHAN ANSWERS:

If I met with this questioner (and question) in person, I might ask, 'Where have you been looking?' Certainly one place I thought it reasonable to 'look' was in churches – not just as architectural delights, but as places where I might gain some certainties. Why is it that some of us who find our way to churches and Christian people and leaders do not find God there? Most likely, we look in these places and to these people, and do not find God, for one of three reasons.

First, because we can get the impression that God is wrapped up somewhere beneath the layers of ritual. And he isn't. I used to think the rituals and 'mysteries' of religious worship were the casket that contained the treasure. But, frankly, much ritual simply makes God yet more inaccessible, and much as we may be drawn to these things, we shouldn't expect them to open the way to God.

Secondly, we may get the impression that the search for God is an interminable intellectual quest. There is nothing wrong with playing 'mind games', but although they will put you in the way of some very clever people, they will not bring you to God.

A third reason church may not lead us to God is because we find we are given moral and ethical instruction, as though a 'better life' was the better way to know God. But, put like that, it isn't.

So I would ask 'Jill', 'what did you discover about the person of Jesus when you made your way to church?' It's the person of Jesus who will supply the answers. Jesus was asked by his disciples on one occasion, 'Lord, show us the Father and that will be enough for us,' to which Jesus replied, 'Anyone who has seen me has seen the Father.' In the next chapter we look at the person of Jesus.

****

Two chapters into *What Christians Believe* and 'Christ' has been little more than a footnote because, as we have seen, not everything that Christians believe is unique to Christianity. Christianity is one of the three major monotheistic faiths (along with Judaism and Islam) and the nature and character of God is revealed in large measure in Scriptures that Jews and Christians hold in common together.

But what marks out Christians from Jews and everyone else is what they believe about Jesus. He is a man who has left a huge and indelible footprint in history. And from what we have read so far we have good reason to believe he holds the key to three questions.

The first concerns the truth about God. The claim of the Bible is that God has revealed himself, as fully as we are able to grasp it, in the person of his Son. So the person of Jesus adds immeasurably to the revelation of God in creation. We dare not ignore that.

The second concerns the truth about judgment. As we have seen, the fact of God removing our ignorance about him makes our failure to honour him as he truly is, worthy of judgment. And in these last verses we have looked at from Paul's teaching in Athens, Jesus is being spoken of as God's appointed judge. (Acts 17:31) We dare not ignore that.

And the third question concerns the hope of rescue from a judgment to come (or 'salvation'). For some, the mention of 'judgment' could seem like a manipulative trick to frighten us into faith in some way. But what if the prospect of judgment is not a cynical trick, but a sober truth? What if that really does make sense in a world where we have robbed our creator God of the honour that is due to him? If that were so, then what we need is the comforting and consoling truth of what Christians believe – which is that Jesus Christ is the means by which God, who is bound to judge, may yet be merciful to us who are guilty.

For these three reasons we must now look at Jesus. We need to 'Mark that man!' and reach a view and verdict about him.

3 Mark that man

Christianity is the only religion in the world
which rests on the person of its founder.

DR GRIFFITH THOMAS

A religion is invariably associated with the person who founded it. But no religion excepting Christianity *rests* on the person who founded it. You may have Judaism without Abraham or Moses, and Islam without Mohammed, Buddhism without the Buddha and Hinduism without Krishna, in a way that you cannot have Christianity without Christ. For at every point Jesus Christ was directing people's attention to himself, not merely as a teacher, but as the subject or focus of everything that he taught.

Jesus says to those who long to find satisfaction in life, 'I am the bread of life. He who comes to me will never go hungry, and he who believes in me will never be thirsty.'[1]

He speaks to those who want to know the right way to and through life, and says, 'I am the light of the world. Whoever follows me will never walk in darkness but have the light of life.'

---

1   This and the following claims are all found in John's Gospel; 6:35; 8:12; 10:11; 11:25; 14:6

He contrasts himself with false spiritual guides of God's people and claims emphatically, 'I am the good shepherd. The good shepherd lays down his life for the sheep.'

He meets two grieving sisters at the graveside of their brother – and his friend – Lazarus and, in the midst of their tears and his, he tells them, 'I am the resurrection and the life. He who believes in me will live, even though he dies; and whoever lives and believes in me will never die.'

Towards the end of his short public ministry, he speaks to his disciples about going to be with his Father God, and explains that belonging to him – Jesus – is the way to the Father for them too. He claims: 'I am the way and the truth and the life. No-one comes to the Father except through me.'

These claims are only a part of an extraordinary catalogue of claims made by Jesus, and by others, for Jesus. There is indeed no Christianity without Jesus Christ. *Christianity is Christ.*[2]

But the revelation of who Jesus is came to his own disciples only very slowly, and the evidence was built up, for the most part, over the period of his three years of public ministry. In the same way today, it is most likely that a settled conviction about the precise identity of Jesus can only come to us slowly as we are exposed to the records of his words and deeds, as the Gospel writers present them to us. To change the analogy, a picture of who Jesus is only emerges as successive pieces of the jigsaw are put in place. Or to use another analogy, if like a jury we are to give an informed verdict concerning the person of Jesus, we need to hear and then weigh the evidence.

---

2   Title of a book by W.H. Griffith Thomas (1861-1924).

Whichever of these analogies we use, what we need is a first-hand account of the words and deeds of Jesus. And that is what the Gospel writers give us.[3] In this chapter we are going to look at the Gospel of Mark, and by exposing ourselves to some of the evidence he brings us, we are going to consider the identity of Jesus. This is how Mark begins his presentation of Jesus to his readers:

[1]The beginning of the gospel about Jesus Christ, the Son of God. [2]It is written in Isaiah the prophet:

'I will send my messenger ahead of you, who will prepare your way – [3]a voice of one calling in the desert, "Prepare the way for the Lord, make straight paths for him."'

[4]And so John came, baptising in the desert region and preaching a baptism of repentance for the forgiveness of sins. [5]The whole Judean countryside and all the people of Jerusalem went out to him. Confessing their sins, they were baptised by him in the Jordan River. [6]John wore clothing made of camel's hair, with a leather belt round his waist, and he ate locusts and wild honey. [7]And this was his message:

'After me will come one more powerful than I, the thongs of whose sandals I am not worthy to stoop down and untie. [8]I baptise you with water, but he will baptise you with the Holy Spirit'.

[9]At that time Jesus came from Nazareth in Galilee and was baptised by John in the Jordan. [10]As Jesus was coming up out of the water, he saw heaven being torn open and the Spirit descending on him like a dove. [11]And

---

3   There are four accounts (or 'Gospels'), one by each of Matthew, Mark, Luke and John. Matthew and John were, it seems, among the twelve disciples that Jesus chose to accompany him during his earthly ministry. Mark and Luke were fellow colleagues of the apostle Paul in his own missionary journeys; Mark – the earliest Gospel writer – very likely received the material for his Gospel from Simon Peter, one of the twelve.

a voice came from heaven: 'You are my Son, whom I love; with you I am well pleased' (Mark 1:1-11).

From these verses (and others that will follow), consider the following seven claims being made for Jesus:

1. The promised Lord

According to Mark, the prophets Malachi and Isaiah[4] tell us that two events lay in the future for God's people at the time at which they were prophesying. The first was the coming of a *messenger* who would prepare the way for the second, which was the coming of *the Lord*: 'I will send my *messenger*...who will... prepare the way *for the Lord*' (vv. 2-3). Mark then tells us, his readers, how those two prophecies have now been fulfilled: the first has been fulfilled in the coming of John the Baptist ('And so John came...' v. 4), and the second has been fulfilled in the coming of Jesus ('At that time Jesus came...' v. 9).

The astonishing fact in all this is that whilst the messenger's role is filled by John the Baptist, the coming of the Lord (for which he was to prepare people) was fulfilled, says Mark, by the coming of Jesus. Mark is saying that Jesus was, and is, 'the Lord' of whom Isaiah spoke. And the Lord, whose coming Isaiah predicted, was none other than the LORD[5] God. Mark is saying *Jesus'* coming fulfils Isaiah's prophecy that the LORD will come – in other words Jesus is the Lord God of this world. It is the most astonishing claim that Mark – or indeed anyone – could possibly make.

---

4   Malachi 3:1; Isaiah 40:3 (Malachi, the last of the Old Testament prophets, was prophesying in the 5th century B.C.; Isaiah in the 8th century B.C.).

5   LORD (in capitals, in our English translations) translates Yahweh, the name by which God revealed himself to Moses, as we saw in chapter 1. (Exod. 3:14).

Of course, for Mark to make this claim doesn't make it true. But it tells us of his conviction as he writes, and indeed the reason for writing as he does. He has a gospel to proclaim – the word 'gospel' means good news – and at the heart of this good news is the person of Jesus, and more particularly his identity as 'the Son of God'. By that phrase *'Son of God'*, he doesn't mean someone *less than* God but the one, who being equally God, is in relationship with God his Father as his only Son. This is confirmed at Jesus' baptism at which, Mark tells us, 'a voice came from heaven: "You are my Son, whom I love; with you I am well pleased"'(v. 11).

Here is the first claim being made for Jesus; he is the *promised Lord*. Here is a second:

2. THE SPIRIT GIVER

⁷And this was [John's] message:

'After me will come one more powerful than I, the thongs of whose sandals I am not worthy to stoop down and untie. ⁸I baptise you with water, but he will baptise you with the Holy Spirit'. (Mark 1:7-8)

John the Baptist's message and ministry were compelling. Notwithstanding his austere lifestyle and the fact that his preaching and baptising took place in the desert region, we read 'the whole Judean countryside and all the people of Jerusalem went out to him' (v. 5). More than that, however, John's preaching convicted the hearts of those who listened, meaning that they did more than give nodding assent to his message; his preaching found them out so that 'confessing their sins, they were baptised by him in the Jordan River'(v. 5).

John's ministry was extraordinarily powerful, both in its breadth (*'all the people* went out to him...') and its depth (*'confessing their sins...'*). Nevertheless, John the Baptist was the first to stress the infinitely superior power and the utterly unique ministry that Jesus would exercise. For John says, 'I baptise you with water, but he [Jesus] will baptise you with the Holy Spirit' (v. 8).

John is saying he could give the sign of water baptism to those who wanted to turn from their sin. But he is also saying that Jesus, by contrast, can give to a person the power of God's Holy Spirit to indwell their lives, and make that turning from sin not just an intention but a reality in life. John, like any preacher, can give the *symbol* of turning to God, but Jesus is the one who can actually give the *substance* of a life turned to God, and lived for him. No wonder John could say 'After me will come one more powerful than I, the thongs of whose sandals I am not worthy to stoop down and untie' (v. 7).

Again, John's claim that Jesus will baptise people with the Holy Spirit — that he is the uniquely powerful Spirit giver — is not a knock-down proof of the identity of Jesus. However, it is consistent with the claim Mark has made (and the case he now builds) that Jesus is none other than God himself, come in the flesh. A third claim follows:

3. THE KINGDOM'S KING

> [14]After John was put in prison, Jesus went into Galilee, proclaiming the good news of God. [15]'The time has come,' he said. 'The kingdom of God is near. Repent and believe the good news!' (Mark 1:14-15).

The Jewish nation of Jesus' time looked forward to the promised kingdom of God. It may by this time in their history have come to be associated with little more than the expulsion of the occupying Roman forces in Israel, and a desire for political autonomy. But historically, Israel's prophets had spoken about the fulfilment of God's purposes for his people, which involved nothing less than God's creation of a 'new heavens and a new earth'.[6] This new creation would be characterised by the presence of God, the absence of suffering and the uninterrupted enjoyment of all God's good gifts by his people for ever. It was a mouth-watering picture of the future which God had promised to give to his people.

At the time Jesus begins his ministry, the faithful among God's people are awaiting that 'kingdom of God'. And it is that hope and expectation that lends great significance to the first recorded words of Jesus' public ministry: 'the time has come.' Literally, the time is 'filled up'. The period of waiting is over. And the reason Jesus can announce that God's longed-for kingdom is about to be established, is because he is the King and he has come to establish that kingdom. With his coming 'the time has come...the kingdom of God is near.'

Of course, we do not yet see the 'new heavens and earth' that the prophets predicted; that is still to come.[7] However, everything Jesus did, everywhere he went in the course of his short earthly ministry, testified to his power over this creation, and anticipated that perfect kingdom, that new heavens and new earth. For Jesus to heal the sick, raise the dead, calm the storm or even turn water into wine – were all different ways of saying 'I am God and I am bringing God's kingdom.'

Again, this claim is not a knock-down proof that Jesus is God come in the flesh. But it is consistent with such

---

6   'Behold, I will create new heavens and a new earth' (Isa. 65:17).

7   In conversation with many Jewish people in north London, where I work, the answer I hear to the question I ask, 'Could Jesus be the promised King of God's people?' is 'No', because when the King (the Messiah) comes, he will eradicate suffering. The claim made by Jesus, and for him, is that the ultimate fulfilment of God's plan of salvation will take place at Jesus' second coming, when an end to suffering will accompany the end of sin (which is invariably behind it). That day of 'salvation' will also be 'the day of judgment'. See further in chapter 7.

a claim. Who else could so confidently proclaim the nearness of God's kingdom, and demonstrate his power over creation in such tangible ways, but the one who was himself in a position to bring God's kingdom to fulfilment?

4. THE LORD OF EVERY MAN

> [16]As Jesus walked beside the Sea of Galilee, he saw Simon and his brother Andrew casting a net into the lake, for they were fishermen. [17]'Come, follow me,' Jesus said, 'and I will make you fishers of men.' [18]At once they left their nets and followed him.
>
> [19]When he had gone a little farther, he saw James son of Zebedee and his brother John in a boat, preparing their nets. [20]Without delay he called them, and they left their father Zebedee in the boat with the hired men and followed him (Mark 1:16-20).

Jesus' claim to bring the kingdom of God is now made explicit in a further way as Jesus here expresses his own authority to call men to follow him.

Here are life-changing encounters for these four fishermen. The key to their lives being changed is – in a word – Jesus. This incident is about Jesus: Jesus' *initiative*, because 'he saw them' (v. 16); Jesus' *authority* because he calls them – 'Come, follow me' (v. 17); Jesus' *promise* which is to empower them – 'I will make you fishers of men' (that is, make them people who will in turn be used to transform many lives); Jesus' *power* which enables them to obey him – 'they followed him' (v. 18); and Jesus' *honour* as they 'left their nets' (v. 18) and 'left their father'(v. 20) to follow him. Here is Mark giving us a picture of Jesus: his initiative, authority, promise, power and honour. In short, Jesus is the rightful Lord of every man.

Once again this is not a knock-down proof of Jesus' identity as God the Son. But it is consistent with it. Jesus' words are not basic moral precepts or proverbial wisdom; he is not here posing simply as a great moral teacher. His words flow from, and point us to, his kingly authority to command the allegiance of us all. 'Come, follow *me* and *I* will make you fishers of men.' It is this same authority that amazes the people in the next recorded incident.

5. THE DEVIL'S DESTROYER

²¹They went to Capernaum, and when the Sabbath came, Jesus went into the synagogue and began to teach. ²²The people were amazed at his teaching, because he taught them as one who had authority, not as the teachers of the law. ²³Just then a man in their synagogue who was possessed by an evil spirit cried out, ²⁴'What do you want with us, Jesus of Nazareth? Have you come to destroy us? I know who you are – the Holy One of God!'

²⁵'Be quiet!' said Jesus sternly. 'Come out of him!' ²⁶The evil spirit shook the man violently and came out of him with a shriek.

²⁷The people were all so amazed that they asked each other, 'What is this? A new teaching – and with authority! He even gives orders to evil spirits and they obey him.' ²⁸News about him spread quickly over the whole region of Galilee (Mark 1:21-28).

It is strange that here, on the lips of a man 'possessed by an evil spirit', comes a very clear testimony to the identity of Jesus. 'I know who you are – the Holy One of God!' The point is that the powers of evil know that their time has come. They are face-to-face with their destroyer. 'What do you want with us, Jesus of Nazareth? Have you come to destroy us?' (v. 24). The answer is that is exactly what Jesus has come to do. 'The reason the Son of God appeared was to destroy the devil's work'(1 John 3:8).

The Bible does not teach 'dualism' – the view that there are two equal and opposite forces (one good and one evil) in the universe, battling it out for supremacy and victory. The Bible teaches the truth of a creator God, who has existed for all time, and who will reign for all eternity. Having said that, the Bible does not ignore the existence of evil either. Indeed, the influence of evil is all-pervasive and sometimes in the biblical record (as in some cultures today), a person is spoken of as 'possessed by an evil spirit'[8] which means, practically speaking, the person possessed is trapped, entirely hostage to the powers of evil. And for him to be free, the evil spirits themselves must be made to submit to a greater power and authority.[9]

Into this situation Jesus steps, as one day he went into the synagogue and began to teach. The people in the synagogue were amazed at his teaching, because he taught them as one who had authority, not as the teachers of the law. But not only were they amazed at his authoritative teaching, but when a man possessed by an evil spirit cries out, Jesus speaks sternly to the evil spirit, 'Be quiet! Come out of him!' (v. 25), whereupon the evil spirit, submitting to Jesus' authority, 'shook the man violently and came out of him with a shriek' (v. 26). Again we read, 'The people were all so amazed that they asked each other, "What is this? A new teaching – and with authority! He even gives orders to evil spirits and they obey him"'(v. 27). No wonder 'news about him spread quickly over the whole region of Galilee' (v. 28).

Once again, it is not a conclusive proof that Jesus is God come in the flesh, but it adds to the growing body of evidence. Jesus is here seen to be superior to the

---

8   See 'Jill asks: What is demon possession?' at the close of this chapter.
9   Mark 3:20-30.

forces of evil, as the creator God must be; Jesus' power over evil, demonstrated in this exorcism, is consistent with his claim to be God.[10] Mark shows us yet more of Jesus' power in the next recorded events.

6. THE DIVINE PHYSICIAN

[29]As soon as they left the synagogue, they went with James and John to the home of Simon and Andrew. [30]Simon's mother-in-law was in bed with a fever, and they told Jesus about her. [31]So he went to her, took her hand and helped her up. The fever left her and she began to wait on them.

[32]That evening after sunset the people brought to Jesus all the sick and demon-possessed. [33]The whole town gathered at the door, [34]and Jesus healed many who had various diseases. He also drove out many demons, but he would not let the demons speak because they knew who he was (Mark 1:29-34).

The medical profession is sometimes spoken of as a 'caring profession', and Jesus' healings certainly demonstrate care and compassion. In the record of an incident that follows soon after this passage above, we read:

[40]A man with leprosy came to him and begged him on his knees, 'If you are willing, you can make me clean.'

[41]Filled with compassion, Jesus reached out his hand and touched the man. 'I am willing,' he said. 'Be clean!' [42]Immediately the leprosy left him and he was cured (Mark 1:40-42).

Jesus' healings show him to be wonderfully compassionate.

But even more strikingly, Jesus' healings demonstrate his creative power. It is because Jesus made us, that he

---

10   See 'Jack asks: 'Why would God create powers of evil?' at the close of this chapter.

can mend us. What else could account for the limitless reach of Jesus' healing ministry? What else except that as the creator God, come in the flesh, he had full power to mend the human beings he had made?[11]

Yet again, it falls short of a conclusive 'proof' that Jesus is God – though by this stage we may well be wondering what a 'conclusive proof' would actually look like – but the evidence of Jesus as the healer of all who came to him, is best explained by the claim that Jesus is indeed God the Son, the creator of all, come to live among us in human form.

7. THE SINNER'S SAVIOUR

[1]A few days later, when Jesus again entered Capernaum, the people heard that he had come home. [2]So many gathered that there was no room left, not even outside the door, and he preached the word to them. [3]Some men came, bringing to him a paralytic, carried by four of them. [4]Since they could not get him to Jesus because of the crowd, they made an opening in the roof above Jesus and, after digging through it, lowered the mat the paralysed man was lying on. [5]When Jesus saw their faith, he said to the paralytic, 'Son, your sins are forgiven.'

[6]Now some teachers of the law were sitting there, thinking to themselves, [7]'Why does this fellow talk like that? He's blaspheming! Who can forgive sins but God alone?'

[8]Immediately Jesus knew in his spirit that this was what they were thinking in their hearts, and he said to them, 'Why are you thinking these things? [9]Which is easier: to say to the paralytic, "Your sins are forgiven," or to say, "Get up, take your mat and walk"? [10]But that you may know that the Son of Man has authority on earth

---

11   See Jill asks: 'Can we really believe in miracles?' at the close of this
     chapter.

to forgive sins...' He said to the paralytic, [11]'I tell you, get up, take your mat and go home.' [12]He got up, took his mat and walked out in full view of them all. This amazed everyone and they praised God saying, 'We have never seen anything like this!' (Mark 2:1-12).

At first sight this episode is simply one more miracle of healing by Jesus, and if that were so it might not add anything to the case that Mark, the Gospel writer, is making for the deity of Jesus – that is, the claim that Jesus is God come in the flesh. But there are two surprises. The first concerns the condition of the paralysed man. The second concerns the claim Jesus makes to meet and mend that condition.

The man's condition, Jesus says, is that he is a sinner. Of course Jesus is not saying this is the only problem; he can see the man is so profoundly paralysed that his four friends have had to carry him to Jesus. Nor is Jesus saying that the man's sin is the cause of the man's paralysis. There may be times when sin does cause sickness,[12] but there is no biblical warrant for automatically seeking a moral or spiritual cause behind a physical defect or sickness. Indeed on one occasion Jesus firmly repudiated such a link.[13] Rather Jesus is identifying this man's deepest need as spiritual – the man is a 'sinner' – rather than physical (his paralysis), as he and his friends surely imagine. So he first addresses this most fundamental issue with the words 'Son, your sins are forgiven' (v. 5). This is the critical issue for all of us, and we explore it in subsequent chapters.

---

12   e.g. 1 Corinthians 11:29-30

13   'As [Jesus] went along, he saw a man blind from birth. His disciples asked him, "Rabbi, who sinned, this man or his parents, that he was born blind?" "Neither this man nor his parents sinned", said Jesus, "but this happened so that the work of God might be displayed in his life."' John 9:1-3.

However, it is a second surprise which drives home Mark's point about Jesus in this part of his Gospel. It is that Jesus is the one who can address the most significant need that this man has. When Jesus claims to be able to forgive the man's sins he is not claiming simply to forgive wrongs done by this man to Jesus personally – indeed there is no evidence of any such wrongs. No, Jesus is claiming to forgive all the wrong that this man has ever done to *anyone*, including to God himself. The teachers of the law sitting there are right to be thinking that to make such a claim is to make a claim to be God. That is why they ask, 'Who can forgive sins but God alone?' (v. 7). It is God's prerogative to forgive our sins, and for a mere man – as the religious leaders assume Jesus to be – to claim to forgive sins is therefore blasphemous and horribly insulting to God.

But that is the question which Jesus, by his words and actions, forces to our attention. Is he just a man? Or is Jesus both man *and God*? Is he blaspheming or does he indeed have the right to forgive sins, as he here claims to do?

Jesus is fully aware of the issue in the minds of his hostile audience. They cannot believe that he might indeed be God; they can only assume he is blaspheming in taking to himself the divine prerogative to forgive sins. Jesus doesn't answer them by simply making a verbal claim to be God, but by *proving* that he has authority to forgive sins. He does this by healing the paralysed man:

[10]'But that you may know that the Son of Man has authority on earth to forgive sins...' He said to the paralytic, [11]'I tell you, get up, take your mat and go home.' [12]He got up, took his mat and walked out in full view of them all. This amazed everyone and they praised God saying, 'We have never seen anything like this!' (Mark 2:10-12)

Jesus' physical and visible healing of the paralysed man becomes the proof of the spiritual, but invisible, healing of this man – the forgiveness of his sins.

So Jesus is indeed not just a miracle worker; he is God come to this world to be the Saviour of sinners – sinners whose primary need in life and at death is the forgiveness of sins that Jesus alone can bring.

WHO IS THIS?

No-one becomes a believer in Jesus without confronting the central question, 'Who is this man?' It was the very question which confronted his earliest followers, and we ourselves cannot avoid it:

> [35]That day when evening came, he said to his disciples, 'Let us go over to the other side.' [36]Leaving the crowd behind, they took him along, just as he was, in the boat. There were also other boats with him. [37]A furious squall came up, and the waves broke over the boat, so that it was nearly swamped. [38]Jesus was in the stern, sleeping on a cushion. The disciples woke him and said to him, 'Teacher, don't you care if we drown?'
>
> [39]He got up, rebuked the wind and said to the waves, 'Quiet! Be still!' Then the wind died down and it was completely calm.
>
> [40]He said to his disciples, 'Why are you so afraid? Do you still have no faith?'
>
> [41]They were terrified and asked each other, 'Who is this? Even the wind and the waves obey him!' (Mark 4:35-41)

From this incident, as so many others, we learn about the humanity of Jesus. He was a man. If you punched him, he would bleed. If you starved him, he would be hungry.

He had a human family of mother and brothers.[14] He experienced temptation. And, as this incident shows, if he experienced physical and mental tiredness he needed to sleep. If our only picture of Jesus has been gleaned from stained-glass windows, we need to know that his feet touched the ground and he really walked this earth as a man. His own favourite title for himself, 'the Son of Man', bears witness, in part, to his humanity.[15]

However, for his disciples who are there with him in a boat on storm-tossed Lake Galilee, his humanity is not in doubt. As he sleeps in the stern, they don't doubt he is a human being, but they don't understand that he is a great deal more. In this incident they are twice terrified. First, they are made very anxious by the storm. It is described as 'a furious squall' (v. 37), and 'the waves broke over the boat so that it was nearly swamped'. It was enough to cause these disciples, some of whom at least were fishermen by trade and must have known rough seas, to wake Jesus and say to him 'Teacher, don't you care if we drown?'

However, the real shock for the disciples is still to come. It is not now the ferocity of the storm, but rather the power of Jesus to calm the storm that causes them deep unease. 'He got up, rebuked the wind and said to the waves, "Quiet! Be still!" Then the wind died down and it was completely calm. He said to his disciples,

---

14 The Bible doesn't teach the perpetual virginity of Mary, the mother of Jesus. It appears she went on to conceive children in the normal way, after the birth of Jesus. (e.g. Mark 3:31).

15 For some of the attentive and discerning of Jesus' Jewish listeners, the 'Son of Man' was also a title used in the book of Daniel, to describe the one who receives divine authority to rule from the 'Ancient of Days': 'In my vision at night I looked, and there before me was one like a son of man, coming with the clouds of heaven. ... He was given authority, glory and sovereign power; all peoples, nations and men of every language worshipped him. His dominion is an everlasting dominion that will not pass away, and his kingdom is one that will never be destroyed.' Daniel 7:13-14.

"Why are you so afraid? Do you still have no faith?" They were terrified and asked each other, "Who is this? Even the wind and the waves obey him!'" (vv. 39-41).

They are not now terrified by the presence of the storm, but by Jesus' calming of the storm. They are in the presence of a man they thought they knew well, but they can't fathom him. Here is a man who is obeyed by the wind and the waves. So, they ask in amazement 'Who is this? Even the wind and the waves obey him!' (v. 41).

For all that the disciples had heard and seen, they do indeed, 'still have no faith' in Jesus as more than a man. Therefore, when Jesus acts as only God could do, speaking to the wind and waves, and commanding their obedience, they are totally unprepared for the immediate response made by the elements. They go from being terrified by the storm to being terrified by the man who can control the wind and waves with a word. They now ask the best of questions – 'Who is this?' – although after all the earlier evidence they might be expected to have some inkling of the answer.

It is a sign that we are taking some of the evidence surveyed here seriously that we too ask the question, 'Who is this?' It is not such a good sign if we feel able to pigeonhole Jesus in the safe category of 'a great man' or 'a good teacher' because, of course, by word and deed he claimed so much more than these things.

The writer C.S. Lewis surveyed the evidence, and concluded:

> I am trying here to prevent anyone saying the really foolish thing that people often say about him: 'I'm ready to accept Jesus as a great moral teacher, but I don't accept his claim to be God.' That is the one thing we must not say. A man who was merely a man and said the sort of things Jesus said would not be

a great moral teacher. He would either be a lunatic – on a level with the man who says he is a poached egg – or else he would be the Devil of hell. You must make your choice. Either this man was, and is, the Son of God: or else a madman or something worse. You can shut him up for a fool, you can spit at him and kill him as a demon; or you can fall at his feet and call him Lord and God. But let us not come with any patronising nonsense about his being a great human teacher. He has not left that open to us. He did not intend to.[16]

'Who is Jesus?' is an *unavoidable* question because, as we have seen, Christianity rests on the person of its founder.

'Who is Jesus?' is an *answerable* question, because Mark in his Gospel, as also Matthew, Luke and John in theirs, gives to us readers the evidence of his words and deeds, so that we may answer this question for ourselves.

'Who is Jesus?' is a *personal* question full of implication for us. If Jesus be God, as the evidence seems to demand, then not only has God revealed himself with perfect clarity in the person of his Son, but the response we make to the person of Jesus will be the response we make to God himself.

Therefore, to reject Jesus is to reject God. But to submit our lives to Jesus is to submit our lives to God. Indeed, the apostle Paul makes clear that to honour *Jesus* is the way we give to *God* the glory due to him:

> [9]Therefore God exalted him [Jesus] to the highest place and gave him the name that is above every other name, [10]that at the name of Jesus every knee should bow, in heaven and on earth and under the earth, [11]and every tongue confess that Jesus Christ is Lord, to the glory of God the Father. (Phil. 2:9-11)

---

16   C.S. Lewis, *Mere Christianity.*

******

BIG QUESTIONS

JILL ASKS:
What is demon possession?

JONATHAN ANSWERS:
In the Gospel accounts it seems there are various individuals spoken of as possessed by one or more evil spirits. And, as we have seen, practically speaking that appears to mean the person is incapable of behaving rationally. But this is part of a bigger picture the Bible paints of the whole of mankind which, turning from the rule of God, comes under the control of the evil one. So the important lesson is that the Bible never confines the work of the devil to those said to be 'possessed', and nor should we. The devil may 'possess' some in a peculiarly shocking way, but he influences all who do not belong to Jesus, and Jesus has come to destroy his work in all its forms and guises (Eph. 2:2; 1 John 3:8).

JACK ASKS:
If evil is not eternally coexistent with God, but a power created by God, why on earth would God create evil?

JONATHAN ANSWERS:
Many will want to know why God would create evil. The Bible's answer is that God did not create evil, but God created all beings, including human and angelic ones, and it seems it was one such angelic being that

chose a path of rebellion against God, and became in turn the source of evil and corruption in the world. If this, rather than 'dualism' described above, is true, then one would expect the creator would have power over this, as every other aspect of his creation. This is indeed seen to be the case – for example in the incident of the casting out of the evil spirit[17], as also in the anticipated judgment to be brought on the devil at the end of time. (Jude 6; Rev. 12:7f.).

JILL ASKS:
Can we really believe in the miracles claimed to have been performed by Jesus?

JONATHAN ANSWERS:
Some people feel they simply cannot believe in miracles. To the extent that such people believe in a creator God, God is understood to have made the world which is 'self-governing' in the sense that it cannot but obey the observable laws of nature, and God himself is powerless to intervene or interfere in the world that he has made. This is a view of the world known as 'deism'.

The Bible, however, reveals a God who has not only made our world, but sustains and controls it (and this is called 'theism'). He does this, for the most part, through what we observe in the 'laws of nature' which empirical scientific research can investigate, corroborate and validate. Needless to say, if this universe did not regularly operate according to such 'laws' of cause and effect, life would be extremely unpredictable for all of us, and the scientists would be out of a job!

The point about Jesus' miracles which we – as the disciples and others who witnessed them – can find so

---

17   see above, 'The devil's destroyer'

difficult is that Jesus appears to 'suspend' the observable laws of nature. But if Jesus *is* the creator God, who himself sustains the world he has made, is he not also free to suspend the observable laws of nature by which he regularly governs this world? If 'not', do we really believe that God can be God in his own world?

If God is God, and if Jesus is God, the Son, entering into the world that he has made, then are we not bound to expect to see Jesus performing 'miracles'?

****

If there is a reason to believe that Jesus is 'the Christ, the Son of God' (as Mark states in the introduction to his Gospel, and John at the close of his), then it is to be found in the eyewitness accounts of his life and ministry, including – as the authors recount – his death and resurrection.

Therefore, the miracles Jesus performed, and that we have begun to look at in Mark's account of the life of Jesus, are not designed to be a stumbling block to faith for reasonable, rational, scientifically minded men and women. Rather, they are given as a stepping stone to faith in Jesus; they are pointers or signs to the identity of Jesus. As Jesus' disciples witnessed him calm the storm, they were put on notice that Jesus was special, and they ask the $64,000 question: 'Who is this man?'

Nonetheless, there are still, for many of us, unanswered questions. Someone might ask, does it not all boil down to 'faith' at the end of the day? And if so, surely one of two consequences follows. Either we are one of the few who take that 'leap of faith', or we remain one of the majority for whom there are no such certainties. But the outcome is two groups that cannot converse. Each person's position seems right to them. But neither position is persuasive for the other. Each is locked into a cycle of thinking from which there is little hope of escape.

Is that right? Is 'faith' really so against reason, or beyond it, that books like this can only ever be 'preaching to the converted'? Is there any solid and substantial reason for those without faith to have faith? That's the question for the next chapter.

Facts or faith?

Jesus did many other miraculous signs in the presence of his disciples, which are not recorded in this book. But these are written that you may believe that Jesus is the Christ, the Son of God, and that by believing you may have life in his name.

JOHN 20:30-31

Faith has got itself a bad press among many people, for two reasons. First, it is widely assumed that faith is a very bad substitute for facts. Faith is seen simply as a matter of building a life on dubious foundations, being rather gullible, a bit soft in the head and fatally vulnerable to wishful thinking. Even where a person is envied for their faith, ('I wish I had your faith'), the unspoken subtext is really 'whilst I wish I had what you gain from your faith – peace, calm, hope – I am glad I am not so stupid as to believe what you actually believe.'

Secondly, 'faith' is seen as changing nothing except a person's own perspective on life. This is what contributes to the view that faith is a crutch; it is a personal, emotional, psychological strength and support for those who find life difficult. But it cannot actually and objectively change a person's situation in life or destination after death. The idea that faith changes anything other than my own personal perception of life is exactly what many people cannot accept. In a recent discussion I have had with one atheist, his very great difficulty with all that I said was

85

that the mere fact of faith should, in the Christian scheme of things, be the key determining factor for how my life would go, now and eternally.

In other words, faith is seen first, as a baseless and groundless personal fantasy, and second, as resulting in certain subjective and unquantifiable benefits for the individual inhabiting that fantastical world of myth and mystery. It is a bit like a placebo; it changes nothing in reality, but it does a lot of good for people who think 'it works'.[1]

---

1   To be fair there are some notable and surprising exceptions to this common outlook of atheists, as, for example, Matthew Parris writing in *The Times* on 27th December 2008, under the title: 'As an atheist, I truly believe Africa needs God – Missionaries, not aid money, are the solution to Africa's biggest problem - the crushing passivity of the people's mindset'. The following is an extract of what he wrote:

'Before Christmas I returned, after forty-five years, to the country that as a boy I knew as Nyasaland. Today it's Malawi, and *The Times* Christmas Appeal includes a small British charity working there. Pump Aid helps rural communities to install a simple pump, letting people keep their village wells sealed and clean. I went to see this work.

It inspired me, renewing my flagging faith in development charities. But travelling in Malawi refreshed another belief, too: one I've been trying to banish all my life, but an observation I've been unable to avoid since my African childhood. It confounds my ideological beliefs, stubbornly refuses to fit my world view, and has embarrassed my growing belief that there is no God.

Now a confirmed atheist, I've become convinced of the enormous contribution that Christian evangelism makes in Africa: sharply distinct from the work of secular NGOs, government projects and international aid efforts. These alone will not do. Education and training alone will not do. In Africa Christianity changes people's hearts. It brings a spiritual transformation. The rebirth is real. The change is good.

I used to avoid this truth by applauding - as you can - the practical work of mission churches in Africa. It's a pity, I would say, that salvation is part of the package, but Christians black and white, working in Africa, do heal the sick, do teach people to read and write; and only the severest kind of secularist could see a mission hospital or school and say the world would be better without it. I would allow that if faith was needed to motivate missionaries to help, then, fine: but what counted was the help, not the faith.

But this doesn't fit the facts. Faith does more than support the missionary; it is also transferred to his flock. This is the effect that matters so immensely, and which I cannot help observing.'

And for the person looking on, therefore, the 'faith phenomenon' appears peculiarly irrelevant. It is only really something of interest to the private thought world of the believer. And increasingly in modern secular Western countries, the private lives of believers are not going to be allowed to shape public, social and political realities. Faith is seen as a private matter which must not intrude into public life. Even politicians who indicate that their public service is shaped by their personal faith are, to that extent, regarded as suspect.

Few topics are as fraught with misunderstanding as a Christian's understanding of 'faith'. What is to be said, from a biblical perspective, by way of response to the suspicion of irrationality attaching to such faith?

EVIDENCE LEADS TO FAITH

The only faith the Bible commends is the faith or belief that flows from facts, for which there is clear evidence.

Faith is not, in the Christian's understanding, something that exists to fill the vacuum created by an absence of knowledge. On the contrary, faith is only possible in the light of what God *has* revealed of himself. As the apostle Paul says, 'faith comes from hearing the message' (Rom. 10:17). If God has *not* spoken to us, we *cannot* put our faith in him. But if God *has* revealed himself through speaking, we *can* put our faith in him.

Faith is therefore a logical response of determining to trust God on account of what God has definitely revealed of himself to us; it is not a wish list for those who feel they are in the dark about what God is like. Faith, as Christians understand it, is a response we make to what we *do* know, and not a calculated guess about what we do *not* know.

Luke writes one of the four accounts we have of the life, death and resurrection of Jesus. What motivates him to write it? He tells us in his opening sentences:

> [1]Many have undertaken to draw up an account of the things that have been fulfilled among us, [2]just as they were handed down to us by those who from the first were eye-witnesses and servants of the word. [3]Therefore, since I myself have carefully investigated everything from the beginning, it seemed good also to me to write an orderly account for you, most excellent Theophilus, [4]so that you may know the certainty of the things you have been taught. (Luke 1:1-4)

Luke writes for Theophilus, who has heard about what Christians believe: he has been taught those things. Some of us can say the same – we can look back on school R.E. or R.S. lessons, or church Sunday school, or our parents' instruction and say, 'these are the things I have been taught'. But the question in our minds is, 'are they true?' Can I be certain I have been taught the truth?

Luke does not simply say, 'believe, believe, believe...' and pour scorn on us doubters. He says something quite different and much more helpful.

First, he says he has made a careful investigation 'of everything from the beginning'. Just pause to note that, at a distance of two millennia from the events in question, *we* cannot do this. We weren't there ourselves. It's illogical for us to pit our wits and second-hand doubts against eyewitnesses and those, like Luke, who compiled detailed accounts within their own lifetimes.

Second, Luke says that his own 'care' in research is for the sake of giving certainty to Theophilus (to whom he writes) and, by extension, to us today. We mustn't overlook the corollary: if Luke's careful research is with the aim of giving us certain knowledge, then our certain knowledge is impossible without his careful research. In other words, certainty is only possible because eyewitness accounts are available.

Jesus' friend and follower, the apostle John, ends the penultimate chapter of his Gospel – quoted at the head of this chapter – in a similar way to that in which Luke begins his Gospel. He explains why he has written his Gospel by saying:

> [30]Jesus did many other miraculous signs in the presence of his disciples, which are not recorded in this book. [31]But these are written that you may believe that Jesus is the Christ, the Son of God... (John 20:30-31)

If you were to ask John, 'on what basis could I possibly become a believer in Jesus?' he would answer, as he does here, 'on the basis of what I have here recorded about what Jesus did'.

Therefore, the route to faith has three significant milestones. First, God has *revealed* himself in the person of Jesus: 'Jesus *did* many ...miraculous signs...' Secondly, John has *recorded* what Jesus did – not all, but enough: 'these are written...' Thirdly, we are invited to *read the record and receive the truth* that John is relaying to us. And as a result of us *receiving* what John has *recorded* of what God has *revealed*, we are able to believe that Jesus is who he claimed to be, that he is 'the Christ, the Son of God'.

So it is the evidence John has gathered that leads to the possibility of faith in Jesus as the Christ. There is no other way to faith in this Jesus. Evidence leads to faith. A number of consequences follow:

First, Christians will be rightly sceptical of claims made by different 'faith communities'. The perspective of someone who does not espouse a particular faith is often that all religions are really teaching the same essential truths, and commending to their adherents the same good life. Invariably, such a view says more about the disinterest of the individual than any real insight of a committed follower. Saying all religions teach essentially the same thing is rather like me (a white Englishman) saying all Chinese babies look the same; it simply means I don't know many Chinese babies at all or any of them very well.

The plain truth is that different religions do teach very different things, and commend significantly different lifestyles. Take the person of Jesus, for example. Islam and Judaism[2] both reject the idea that Jesus is God come in human form. Islam rejects that Jesus is the Son of God. Judaism rejects that Jesus is the Messiah – God's 'Christ' or anointed king. Islam rejects that Jesus died on the cross, and Judaism rejects that Jesus' death on the cross is the way of salvation.[3] Muslims, Christians and Jews are not necessarily close to one another because they are all 'people of faith', as though there was a virtue in 'faith' regardless of what is believed.

Christians, therefore, are not sentimental about faith, as though there were really no significant differences between 'faiths' or as if any faith were automatically better than none. Christians do not necessarily have more in common with those who espouse a different faith than with those who claim they have none. No, Christians are what they are because of what they have read of what the authors of Scripture have recorded of what God has revealed, and we do not think that being a Hindu, Buddhist, Muslim or Sikh is the next best thing! On the contrary, the call to believe the Christian

---

2   Of course very many of the first Christians were Jews (see, for example, Acts 21:20 'thousands of Jews [Greek word 'myriads'] have believed'), and still today many of Jewish background and descent come to put their trust in Jesus as the long-awaited Jewish 'Messiah' (Hebrew) or 'Christ' (Greek). If what Christians believe is correct, the *true* Jew is a believer in Jesus as the Christ. 'Judaism' does not teach that Jesus is the Christ.

3   See chapter 6.

message is accompanied by strong warnings not to believe myths and old wives' tales.[4]

Secondly, it is a mistake to identify only some people as 'people of faith', and apply the label of ostrich-like irrationality to them alone. As we saw in our look at the apostle Paul's words to the Athenians,[5] the Bible would say that *all* men and women are people of faith, in the sense that we are all ascribing ultimate value or worth to something or someone, and serving – or worshipping – that person or thing. I might be yielding my life in the service of (=worshipping) a career, or a relationship, or physical fitness, or material prosperity or just a reputation for being a wonderful person, liked by all.

Therefore, when the Christian message is proclaimed, it is not envisaged that people who believe are becoming people of faith at that time, but that people who believe the message about Jesus are *changing* the direction of their lives from the service of the gods or idols that they have hitherto worshipped, to the service of the one true God. The only real issue for all people is not whether to be people of faith – we all are people of faith whether we like it or not – but whether to worship the only One who is indeed worthy of the adoration of our hearts and lives.

One way, then, of describing the natural condition of all mankind is to say that our minds are no longer captive to the truth about God, and that in consequence our lives are no longer devoted to him. The Bible is saying futile thinking leads to foolish living; we 'have exchanged the truth of God for a lie, and worship and serve created things rather than the Creator'(Rom. 1:25). The lie we believe is that there is no creator God to be worshipped; living that lie will involve, in various ways, making the good gifts of our creator God the object of our worship.

---

4   'Have nothing to do with godless myths and old wives' tales' (1 Tim. 4:7).

5   See chapter 2, and Acts 17.

Therefore, the process of turning to God involves, for every person, receiving the truth about God (rather than suppressing that truth[6]) and serving this living and true God (rather than the idols our hearts have cherished till now). For this reason the Christians at Thessalonica in the first century A.D. were spoken of as those who had 'turned to God from idols to serve the living and true God...'(1 Thess. 1:9) Indeed, that is the truth about anyone who becomes a Christian. They believe the truth about God, rather than a lie, and they serve this true and living God, rather than an idol.

Therefore, the Bible does not advocate exaggerated respect for the observably religious. If their religion is anything other than that which God has revealed through his Son, it will be error not truth, needing correction not approval. Nor are those who consider themselves irreligious to be too smug about those poor simple people who need a religious faith that they themselves do not. Everyone has a view of reality, and someone or something of ultimate value that is served or worshipped; that is a religion. For all of us, the truth must correct the lies we believe, and the true and living God must supplant the idols we serve.

The way that will happen for all of us is for our minds, fully engaged, to be attentive to the evidence concerning Jesus that leads to faith in him. 'These are written that you may believe that Jesus is the Christ, the Son of God...' *Evidence leads to faith.*

FAITH LEADS TO LIFE

If the first criticism of the Christian faith is that it is groundless (without a basis in fact), the second criticism is that it is useless (without a benefit for life – or death).

---

6   Romans 1:18, see further in chapter 5.

We need to digress for a moment, because in the minds of those who reject faith in Jesus Christ, on account of the fact that faith in him would 'change nothing', this observation is believed to be an entirely negative assertion. Why bother with a faith that doesn't change anything? If it changes nothing, it is worth nothing.

But a moment's reflection tells us that even if it were true that faith in Jesus changes nothing (and that's the main question we'll come to in a moment), it would not for that reason alone be as suspect or worthless as might be supposed. The alternative could be a whole lot more suspect. Imagine, for example, that all Christians automatically became rich or healthy, or found the perfect marriage partner, or developed the most glittering social circle of friends, acquaintances and contacts. Imagine how suspect belonging to Christ and his people would be if there were just such a link between going to church and becoming well connected, rich, influential, famous and desirable as a marriage partner.

If such consequences followed, one can see how many would be drawn to Jesus, and his church, but equally one would have a whole lot more sympathy for the sceptics who would conclude that whilst Christianity is not true, the church is 'a great club' to which to belong.

So to the extent it is true that being a Christian guarantees no change for the better in my own temporal circumstances – and indeed that in some respects they are bound to worsen[7] – we can be glad; if it did guarantee a change for good in my circumstances, faith would

---

7   'In fact, everyone who wants to live a godly life in Christ Jesus will be persecuted...' (2 Tim. 3:12).

be suspect.[8] The Christian church is surely right not to want to grow 'rice-Christians', that is, people who will sign up to the faith not out of conviction that it is true, but because of some particular (albeit unrelated) advantage that will follow – 'a bowl of rice', 'a place at a church school', 'a useful group of business contacts', 'a wedding in a pretty church building'.

But having said that, John in his Gospel claims not only that there is a basis for faith in facts, but also that there is a point and a purpose to faith in Jesus. John echoes Jesus in telling us that faith in Jesus ('that he is the Christ') leads to *life*, '...that by believing you may have life in his name' (John 20:31). More specifically, two key words identify aspects of life that are enjoyed only by the believer, 'Relationship' and 'Resurrection'.

RELATIONSHIP

The first aspect of the life that Jesus gives a person who has faith in him is 'relationship'. The really precious part of life, as we all discover sooner or later, is relationships, and the most important and satisfying relationship for which we have been made is a relationship with God.

If 'eternal life' sounds rather airy-fairy, Jesus is quite specific about what this means in practice:

---

8   It is a theme explored in the book of Job. 'The Lord said to Satan, "Have you considered my servant Job? There is no-one on earth like him; he is blameless and upright, a man who fears God and shuns evil." "Does Job fear God for nothing?" Satan replied. "Have you not put a hedge around him and his household and everything he has? You have blessed the works of his hands, so that his flocks and herds are spread throughout the land. But stretch out your hand and strike everything he has, and he will surely curse you to your face."' (Job 1:8-11). Satan's taunt is that Job is a believer in God for the sake of the good things God gives and guarantees to him. God, through Job, proves Satan wrong.

Now this is eternal life: that they may know you, the only true God, and Jesus Christ, whom you have sent (John 17:3).

Although we have all been made by God and for God, we cannot now presume to be in a right relationship with God.[9] But it is fundamental to the life we receive through Jesus that the relationship with God, for which he made us, is restored by Jesus.[10]

The nature of this relationship is clarified in Scripture. First, it is essentially a relationship with God as *Father*. When I belong to Jesus, God's one and only Son, I am adopted into God's family. I become a child in God's family, and he becomes my Father. The apostle John declares:

'To all who received [Jesus], to those who believed in his name, he gave the right to become children of God – children born not of natural descent, nor of human decision or a husband's will, but born of God' (John 1:12).

Note that although God is everywhere spoken of as our creator, the Bible does not generally speak of us as his children; the privilege of being a child in the Father's family, as opposed to simply being a creature in God's creation, is reserved for those who belong to Jesus. He alone can bring us to God as Father. As Jesus says elsewhere,

'I am the way and the truth and the life. No-one comes to the Father except through me' (John 14:6).

Secondly, this relationship is characterised by communication, and this is two-way. When I am adopted into

9   See chapter 5.
10   See chapter 6.

God's family and have God as my Father, the wonderful truth is that I can talk to God as Father and know that he hears me. Of course, because God is God, omnipotent and omnipresent, he can hear everything. But for the child of God, there is access into God's presence at any and every time to talk to him, and it is a communication that he delights to receive.

On one occasion after Jesus has been praying, his disciples ask him to teach them to pray. How will Jesus reply? How will he teach them to enter into the presence of God in such a way that they can be assured of being heard? What posture – sitting, kneeling, prostrate or standing? What place – a quiet room, a synagogue, a temple or a place of beauty in nature? And in what way – with candles and incense or with words or songs or in silence? There were surely so many possible areas on which he might instruct them.

What is striking is the stark simplicity of Jesus' reply: 'When you pray, say: "Father..."'(Matt. 6:9). The disciple of Jesus has immediate access through Jesus into the presence of God as Father, not by the mastery of religious technique, but by the gift of being made a child of God and being adopted into his family. Such children always have access to their Father.

The story is told of how, during the American Civil War, a soldier sat on a bench outside the White House looking distressed. A little boy came by and asked him what was wrong. The soldier said he needed to see the President, but that he had been denied access. Hearing this, the boy took him by the hand and led him straight into President Lincoln's office. Addressing the President, the boy said, 'Father, this soldier really needs to speak with you.' A son generally has access to his father, and what is generally true humanly is definitely true spiritually.

And this communication with the Father is not only possible for the child of God, but it is also infinitely desirable. So, the apostle Paul says to the believers in Jesus in Rome,

> ...you received the Spirit of sonship [or adoption]. And by him we cry, 'Abba, Father'. The Spirit himself testifies with our spirit that we are God's children. (Rom. 8:15)

Talking to the Father is not the awkward communication of a citizen to a remote sovereign, but the natural cry of a child to his or her father, that wells up from within the child and assumes (rightly) that he/she will be received and the request will be heard.

But the privilege of communication with God as Father is not only the privilege of talking *to* the Father but of hearing *from* him. This is even more wonderful! It is good to know my heavenly Father will listen to me, but it is even better to know he has things to say to me. And he has! He speaks to me as his child. He speaks to me also as a member of his church; much of the New Testament is God speaking to his people corporately, rather than to individual members of a local church.

And God's Word to me in the pages of Scripture will fulfil two tasks; it will point me to Jesus so that I am established in my faith in Jesus and experience the salvation he brings, and it will equip me to serve God with my life. Established and equipped; saved to serve. All this will be the fruit of God, my Father, speaking to his people, and to me as one of his children.

A third aspect of the relationship that God intends for me is hinted at in what we have seen here about the way God speaks to me. When God graciously makes me his child, he brings me into his family and

I acquire a multitude of brothers and sisters. Jesus acknowledged this 'family of his Father' for himself. 'Whoever does God's will is my brother and sister and mother'(Mark 3:34). And the same great privilege attaches to all those for whom God is Father. All those who are children of this same heavenly Father have all his children for their spiritual family. And a sign of being in a living relationship with God as Father, is that I acknowledge the Father's family and love its members.

> Dear friends, let us love one another, for love comes from God. Everyone who loves has been born of God and knows God. (1 John 4:7)

Indeed, love for God, and love for his adopted children are so closely linked in Scripture and in human experience, that

> If anyone says, 'I love God,' yet hates his brother, he is a liar. For anyone who does not love his brother, whom he has seen, cannot love God, whom he has not seen. (1 John 4:20)

Here, then, is the first sense in which faith in Jesus leads to *life*. I come into relationship with God as my heavenly Father. This relationship with God as Father is one in which he invites me to speak to him in prayer and he speaks to me through his Word. At the same time, I become part of his family, and the assurance that I am loved by him will increase as I experience the love of his people – and as I, in turn, commit to loving them.

RESURRECTION

Believers in Jesus receive new life and, as we have seen, much of this is experienced in the present. But the word 'resurrection', describing a second aspect of the *life* that flows from faith in Jesus, is a reminder of the Bible's claim that a good deal of the life that comes to the Christian lies in the future. The apostle Paul wrote to the Christians at Corinth, 'If only for this life we have hope in Christ, we are to be pitied more than all men' (1 Cor. 15:19).

Why are we to be 'pitied'? Partly because the resurrection of Christ and of Christians stand or fall together. In an unexpected flow of the argument, the apostle Paul explains that if we are not to be raised from the dead, then Christ has not been raised either. And if Christ has not been raised, then all that is claimed by him and for him also falls away. In which case all that Christians proclaim (in terms of the possibility of knowing God through Christ) is useless, and faith in Jesus indeed accomplishes nothing, just as some suggest (then and now).

Further, without a full confidence in Jesus for the future we are pitiable, for the earthly life of the Christian will often be hard. Indeed, it will sometimes lead to an early grave. An estimated 200 million Christians in sixty countries are now suffering increasing victimisation.[11] And it is indeed pitiable to lose an earthly life, out of loyalty to Christ, in circumstances where the grave is just a dead end.

We are bound to ask, can Christ's people be confident in a resurrection from the dead? At the graveside of a man named Lazarus, Jesus meets two grieving sisters to whom he makes the astonishing claim,

---

11   The thirty worst countries for persecution have been listed as 1. North Korea 2. Saudi Arabia 3. Iran 4. Somalia 5. Maldives 6. Yemen 7. Bhutan 8. Vietnam 9. Laos 10. Afghanistan 11. Uzbekistan 12. China 13. Eritrea 14. Turkmenistan 15. Comoros 16. Chechnya 17. Pakistan 18. Egypt 19. Burma 20. Sudan (North) 21. Iraq 22. Azerbaijan 23. Brunei 24. Cuba 25. Qatar 26. Libya 27. Nigeria (North) 28. Djibouti 29. India 30. Sri Lanka

[25]I am the resurrection and the life. He who believes in
me will live, even though he dies; [26]and whoever lives
and believes in me will never die. (John 11:25-26)

The claim to be 'the resurrection and the life' carries
two consequences; the first is addressed to those who
die physically before Jesus Christ returns to this world
as its Saviour and Judge at the end of the age. All those
who have died, 'believing in' – that is belonging to –
Jesus, will be raised from the dead at Jesus' return, he
says. The second consequence is addressed to those who
remain alive when Jesus returns at the end of the age.
All those who are alive at that time and are found to
believe in Jesus will never die.

'I am the resurrection and the life' – it's a magnificent
claim Jesus makes, and these are breathtaking consequences. We must distinguish what Jesus here claims
to do for those who trust in him, from what many people
think is on offer after death for all people.

First, resurrection is quite different from reincarnation. Those who believe in reincarnation are apt
to think that the quintessential 'me' (my soul or spirit)
lives on after death, but in another body (that is, in
another living creature). This idea falls well short of the
glorious comfort and certain hope which the believer in
Jesus can have concerning the future. Equally, it appears
to offer something easier to bear than the destruction
that the New Testament warns is waiting for those
who reject God and salvation through his Son. One
may be able to see the appeal of reincarnation, but we
need to acknowledge that, unlike the Christian hope
of resurrection, there is not a jot of evidence for this
teaching.

Second, the resurrection of the body, of which
Jesus speaks, also stands in marked contrast to the
immortality of the soul. This latter idea owes a great

deal to a Greek view of man as divisible into separable parts of body and soul. According to this view, when the body dies, the 'soul' or 'spirit' escapes the body in which it has been trapped, to enjoy the unalloyed pleasure of communion with God without the hindrance of pain or the distraction of desire which come with having a body. Again the appeal is obvious. This idea appears to offer the hope of salvation to all, since on this view the soul is immortal, as God is, and nothing can impede the intimate union of the soul of man with the Spirit of God. But again it looks to be a false trail and an empty hope.

In contrast to this view, the Hebrew and biblical understanding of man is not that he has a soul trapped in a body (from which body the soul is liberated at death), but that in his flesh he has the capacity to have fellowship with his maker so that at death he needs a resurrected body.

The reason why the judgment of death is devastating for man is not only because a dead man cannot enjoy life as we know it 'on earth', but because a dead man cannot have fellowship with his creator 'in heaven'. A dead man cannot praise God from the grave.[12]

That is why the prospect of the resurrection of the body, such as Jesus himself experienced, and which is promised to all who belong to Jesus, is such good news. It means I shall have a body, and therefore a capacity to relate to God beyond the grave. This confidence of the believer was expressed long ago in the Bible book of Job:

> [25]I know that my redeemer lives, and that in the end he will stand upon the earth. [26]And after my skin has been destroyed, yet in my flesh I will see God. (Job 19:25-26)

---

12   For example, Psalm 6:5: 'No-one remembers you when he is dead. Who praises you from the grave?'; See also Psalm 30:9, Isaiah 38:18.

This confidence in the resurrection of the body comes to full flowering following the resurrection of Jesus from the dead.[13] Real life comes to light not through mere man-made ideas that we have an indestructible soul, but rather through Christ Jesus 'who has destroyed death and has brought life and immortality to light through the gospel' (2 Tim. 1:10). That gospel includes the good news Jesus taught, that those who belong to him shall enjoy resurrection bodies – as he himself did.

'Faith' is easy to ridicule as groundless and to parody as pointless. But faith in Jesus is neither. It is not groundless; it has a basis in the evidence regarding Jesus: he is a real figure of history, and we have a significant and substantial record of his life, death and resurrection. Neither is faith in Jesus pointless; it leads to *life:* the life of a new relationship (with God as Father), and the life of resurrection to a bodily existence beyond the grave in a new creation. That is a real life, really worth having. And it is on offer to all those who belong to Jesus.

As the apostle John says,

> [30]Jesus did many other miraculous signs in the presence of his disciples, which are not recorded in this book. [31]But these are written that you may believe that Jesus is the Christ, the Son of God, and that by believing you may have life in his name. (John 20:30-31)

Facts lead to faith. And faith leads to life.

******

---

13   See Jack's question at the close of this chapter.

A BIG QUESTION

JACK ASKS:
You talk about the 'resurrection of Jesus from the dead'. I don't believe in it. If the resurrection of Jesus is central to what you think Christianity is about, there is not much point in us talking further to one another about it.

JONATHAN ANSWERS:
I have in mind a number of people who have made this fundamental objection to what Christians believe. It seems at first sight to be an unanswerable riposte: 'you say Jesus rose from the dead; I can't or don't believe that happened'.

Behind this comment there is often – and happily – an enviable amount of common sense. In contrast to a good deal of baseless speculation in spiritual matters, it is a relief to find people making the plain observation from experience that 'dead men don't rise', and to draw the seemingly reasonable conclusion, therefore, that Jesus didn't rise from the dead.

Is there any answer that can be given? At first sight the answer is 'no'. Christians who believe in the historical and bodily resurrection of Jesus from the dead are thought, by some, to believe in something that is really 'unbelievable' by rational, scientifically minded, twenty-first-century people. Believers in the resurrection of Jesus ('the resurrection') are thought to be going *against* reason, or so far *beyond* reason, that others are simply not willing to be complicit in their reckless combination of gullibility and guesswork. Who in their right minds would ditch the reasonable mind for a kind of irrational magic?

In fact, two consequences follow from this stand-off between what is thought to be grounded reason versus the flights of fanciful faith. The first is that few bother to try to persuade believers in the resurrection out of their belief. This may be partly because we want to 'respect' other people's beliefs, but it will be partly because if a person's belief is not sustained by reason, it will probably not be challenged by reason either. Looking back over thirty years, I cannot recall many – if any – trying to reason me out of my belief. My friends will surely think 'what is the point in trying to *reason* with him?'

The second consequence is that few unbelievers in the resurrection can be reasoned into faith. This is not because belief in the resurrection is *necessarily unreasonable* but because reason can only take you so far – not far enough to make a person a believer in the resurrection. All rational people must carry a strong presumption against the resurrection because, in Bible times as now, the plain observable fact of existence, amply supported presumably by biological and medical data, is that dead people do not 'rise from the dead' and return to life.

Are we to conclude then that believers and unbelievers in the resurrection have nothing to say to one another on this topic beyond stating their own – ultimately unverifiable – positions? Certainly, no-one is likely to be bullied, mentally or verbally, into or out of believing, but in this book on 'what Christians believe' the reasonableness of that position needs explaining, and the apparent reasonableness of the 'unbeliever's' position needs questioning. I would do that in the following way:

1. **Christians believe in the resurrection not because there is *final proof*, but because there is *reasonable evidence*.**

After science and maths 'A' levels, I studied, trained and practised law. These different disciplines of science and law tend to use different terminology. Scientists and mathematicians tend to be happy with the concept of *proof;* they start with a hypothesis which by experiment and trial they work to prove or disprove. Very neat.

These scientific methods are less effective, however, in establishing the truth in other areas – historical events for example. Maths and science cannot tell us whether William the Conqueror won the Battle of Hastings.

Lawyers – especially in areas of civil litigation and criminal law – are seeking to establish the truth about events in the past. Although they use the language of 'proof', they really never mean that any event in the past is proved conclusively. They use different 'burdens of proof', meaning that the truth must be established with a greater or lesser degree of certainty depending on the circumstances. In criminal cases a charge brought must usually be proved 'beyond reasonable doubt'; a civil case must usually be proved 'on a balance of probabilities'.

In determining whether Jesus Christ rose from the dead, we need the lawyer's disciplines, not the scientist's ones. We need to ask not 'where is the proof?' but 'what is the evidence?'

2. What is the evidence for the resurrection of Jesus?

As a law student at Bristol University in the late 1970s, I was helped by friends and two of my law lecturers – both believers in the resurrection – to explore the Christian faith. On this issue of the resurrection, I was particularly helped by meeting an eminent lawyer, Professor Sir Norman Anderson,[14] and hearing a talk he gave along the lines of what he had already put into print a decade earlier, entitled 'The Evidence for the Resurrection'.

In this talk and booklet, he first identifies the primary documentary evidence, the written testimony of six witnesses – Matthew, Mark, Luke, John, Paul and Peter. He then comments on the 'strides that modern research has made in determining the date and authorship of these written records' and concludes:

> What about this evidence? It is extremely early – much of it dates back to the very first decade of the Christian era. Thus, the evidence is contemporary and must, at least, be accepted as the substantial record of eye-witnesses.[15]

On the face of it, here is a substantial collection of documentary evidence to make the case for the resurrection. The evidence can perhaps be summarised in three propositions:

---

14   Sir Norman Anderson, OBE, QC, was a distinguished lawyer in his day: Professor of Oriental Laws (1954-1975) and Director of the Institute of Advanced Legal Studies, University of London (1959-1976). He was also a Christian – someone who made a special study of the evidence for the resurrection and came to believe in it. His faith was sorely tested. He and his wife Pat lived to see their three adult children die. One of them, their son Hugh, was a brilliant student at Cambridge University. He died aged 21 from cancer. A few days later, Professor Anderson gave the *Thought for the Day* talk on Radio 4. Giving the talk, he explained that he was convinced that God raised Jesus from the dead. And he added these words: 'On this I am prepared to stake my life. In this faith my son died after saying: "I'm drawing near my Lord." I am convinced that he was not mistaken.'

15   *The Evidence for the Resurrection,* by J.N.D. Anderson.

a. The tomb where the body of Jesus was laid was empty.

The tomb where Jesus was laid was guarded, precisely because the Jewish leaders had picked up rumoured predictions of a resurrection.[16] They were understandably eager not to allow any talk of resurrection to gain credence in circumstances where the real explanation was that the body had been stolen by grave robbers or even deceptive disciples.

Knowing that the tomb was guarded, we struggle to establish who might have had the *motive* and the *opportunity* to steal the body. Neither Jewish nor Roman authorities had the *motive*, even if by collaborative effort they had the *opportunity* to make their way past the guard to steal the body.

And the disciples really had neither opportunity nor motive to steal the body. It seems psychologically implausible that they could steal the body and then be willing to die for the lie that Jesus had risen.

It is difficult, then, to come up with an alternative explanation for the empty tomb other than his bodily resurrection. Not only was the tomb empty, but no-one ever produced Jesus' dead body. Both Jewish and Roman authorities had a vested interest in refuting the claim that Jesus had risen from the dead, and putting an end to the preaching of the resurrection, and yet neither ever produced Jesus' dead body to do so.

---

16   Matthew 27:62-66

b.   The resurrection appearances of Jesus.

The apostle Paul writes concerning Jesus

> [4]...that he was buried, that he was raised on the third day according to the Scriptures, [5]and that he appeared to Peter, and then to the Twelve. [6]After that, he appeared to more than five hundred of the brothers at the same time, most of whom are still living, though some have fallen asleep. [7]Then he appeared to James, then to all the apostles, [8]and last of all he appeared to me also, as to one abnormally born. (1 Cor. 15:4-8)

These appearances need an explanation, and the most natural explanation is indeed that Jesus has risen from the dead. Thomas (one of the twelve disciples) sounds like the voice of sweet reason when, on hearing from the others that they had seen Jesus raised from the dead, he replied:

> 'Unless I see the nail marks in his hands and put his finger where the nails were, and put my hand into his side, I will not believe it'. (John 20:25)

According to the record, Thomas got the evidence he sought:

> [26]A week later [Jesus'] disciples were in the house again, and Thomas was with them. Though the doors were locked, Jesus came and stood among them and said, 'Peace be with you!' [27]Then he said to Thomas, 'Put your finger here; see my hands. Reach out your hand and put it into my side. Stop doubting and believe.' [28]Thomas said to him, 'My Lord and my God!'(John 20:26-28)

Thomas' sight of the risen Jesus leads him to faith in Jesus' resurrection, but Jesus' closing words to Thomas ('stop doubting and believe') don't congratulate him for 'sweet reason' but gently chide him for stubborn incredulity. Jesus is gracious in giving to Thomas the opportunity to make sight the basis for faith but, as Jesus goes on to say, the blessing that accompanies believing is by no means to be dependent on seeing:

> Then Jesus told him, 'Because you have seen me, you have believed; blessed are those who have not seen and yet have believed.' (John 10:29)

c. The changed lives of the disciples.

In his *Evidence for the Resurrection,* J.N.D. Anderson asks: 'What changed the little company of sad and defeated cowards into a band of irresistible missionaries who turned the world upside down because no opposition could deter them?'

It's a fair question. What best explains the change in these men, the birth of the church and the mission and ministry in which they engaged? An answer is needed to that question.

For all that Jesus had taught his disciples that he would rise from the dead, they did not understand him or expect it. (Mark 8:32; 9:10, 32) That being so, his death really was the end for them as they supposed it was for him.

What changed them, so that Peter, for example, could stand up and declare – in the teeth of fierce opposition and a command not to speak or teach at all in the name of Jesus – 'We cannot help speaking about what we have seen and heard' (Acts 4:20)? Is it not reasonable to say that they were changed by their reasonable conviction that Jesus had indeed been raised from the dead?

3. Is it not reasonable to believe in the resurrection?

In the final analysis, the reason people believe in the resurrection of Christ from the dead is not because of any powers of reasoning, but because of the written record or 'revelation' of the Bible.

I believe in the resurrection, not because as a lawyer I have carefully weighed and analysed all the evidence, or indeed because I have carefully weighed, and found wanting, all the objections to the biblical witnesses – though in my judgment the evidence looks solid and the objections look flawed. I believe in the resurrection because it is a part of the larger message of the Bible that we are considering in these pages.

In the broad context of the message of the Bible, I ask myself is it reasonable to suppose Jesus rose from the dead 'on the third day'. And my answer is 'yes' for the following reasons:

a. Because God is God

If there is an all-powerful creator God, such as we have considered earlier, a God who can create something out of nothing – and not just 'something' but life itself – is it not also possible that he can raise a man from the dead?

When the apostle Peter in an early sermon says 'God raised him from the dead...' (Acts 2:24; 3:15) do I find myself saying God couldn't do such a thing? No, I don't. And if I *did* say such a thing, would I not really be questioning my confidence in an all powerful creator God? Would I not be saying 'God, I believe you can do anything, *except* raise the dead?' And would that be a *reasonable* belief? 'Why should any of you consider it incredible that God raises the dead?' (Acts 26:8).

b. Because Jesus is God

Of course, in considering the resurrection of Jesus, we are not asking whether God could raise 'any man' from the dead, but whether the God-Man Jesus rose from the dead. And put like that, it becomes at least as problematic *not to believe* in the resurrection as to do so.

If, as we have begun to see, Jesus was God come in the flesh, then is it not easier to say, along with the apostle Peter '...it was impossible for death to keep its hold on him' (Acts 2:24)? Is not the real mystery that God appeared to give to men the power to 'kill the author of life' (Acts 3:15), as Peter calls Jesus, rather than that 'God raised him from the dead'?

c. Because God who creates life defeats death

It is, as we noted, an observable fact of life that we all die. So it looks as though, in the end, the great creator of life is defeated – because all to whom he gives life lose it at death.

The message of the Bible tells a different story. It says that whilst in our world death is normal (for reasons we will see in the next chapter), death is not natural. We were not made to die even though, as a result of God's judgment of the human race, we now all do so. Death is an intruder into God's world or, to use the apostle Paul's language, death is an 'enemy'. When he goes on to say 'the last enemy to be destroyed is death' (1 Cor. 15:26), he speaks about what God in Christ will accomplish.

The resurrection of Christ, therefore, is not a one-off freak and unbelievable event in history, but the precursor to the resurrection of all God's people in the end. The message of the Bible is that for all

111

God's people, death will ultimately prove to be an utterly defeated enemy.

******

A one sentence summary of the truth we have looked at in this chapter would be that *the creator God is able to give life to those who have faith in his Son, Jesus*. But this kind of summary is reminiscent of the piece of graffiti someone had scribbled on a wall which read 'Jesus is the answer.' Underneath, and in response to this, someone else had scribbled, 'What's the question?' That's the theme of the next chapter. If 'Jesus is the answer', or the solution, we need to know what kind of problem he came to fix. We need to know what is so badly wrong with the world that it has needed the creator God, to come in person to fix it.

5 What's gone wrong with the world?

The most painful of inspired Scriptures

C. H. SPURGEON
(Commenting on Romans 1)

It is clear to almost all of us that there is a great deal wrong with the world. When some friends visited me from another part of the country, and read my local newspaper, they concluded that I lived somewhere they would not choose to live. But doubtless the compliment could be returned! Whether we read or listen to local, national or international news, it sounds as though few places are peaceful, and few situations are safe. Our perception is often that the world is getting worse; more likely, with greater news coverage, we are just more conscious of the way things are.

So we may want to ascribe glory and majesty to the creator God, and we may in our hearts be convinced by Jesus' claims too. But, if so, we are bound to ask what on earth has happened to that good world that God in heaven has made? We're back to that age-old question 'Can I honestly believe in a God of love in a world of suffering?'[1] Sometimes the question is a smokescreen;

---

1 See 'Jill asks' at the close of chapter 1, for an early consideration of this question.

it puts the Christian believer on the back foot and a cynical questioner has a perfect excuse to evade the claims of Christ. But not always. Indeed, in the main, the fact of suffering is a problem for the believer in a good and powerful God – not the unbeliever.

Some years ago, we were hearing a great deal on the news about the abduction of a young girl, Madeleine, from a holiday complex in Portugal. She was asleep in her bed, while her parents were having a meal. A great many people shared in a small way in the distress of the girl's parents. This could have happened to them, and their daughter, on their own idyllic summer holiday. Think of the questions going through people's minds. What will this little girl have suffered? Is the little girl dead? How did she die? What fear, what pain, and what terrible things will she have endured in her last moments? Or is she alive, and suffering the ongoing mental torture of not knowing where her parents are, or whether she will ever see them again? Where is she? Where is she? Where is she?

There was criticism levelled by some at the amount of media attention given to this one case of innocent suffering. The criticism was not on account of the exaggeration of the suffering of the girl, her siblings or her parents; all that was understood and was undeniable. No, the criticism of the reporting was that so much media attention was given to this one case of suffering, when the reality is that terrible things like that, and worse, are happening all over the world all the time. The misleading impression given by the reportage was that this was exceptional suffering. The sad truth is that it is commonplace. Welcome to our world.

The suffering in our world leads to a blame culture. When so much is so wrong, when so many suffer so much and we are powerless to change our lot, we cast around to blame someone for our suffering. We may blame governments and politicians. Certainly we live in an age when government increases its reach further into people's lives because we insist that our governments take responsibility for our well-being in so many areas of life, and take the *blame* when things go wrong.

And where governments can't go, cameras often can. In England we have more CCTV cameras per head of population than any other country in the world, and the aim is to ensure that the antisocial and the criminal take the *blame*.

But where did this antisocial behaviour come from? Perhaps the *blame* for antisocial behaviour can fairly be laid at the door of marriage breakdowns, absentee fathers and poor parenting.

But parents can *blame* architects and town planners who have designed and built 'housing' (tower blocks) that destroys social cohesion.

And town planners can point beyond their area of responsibility to the *failure* of immigration controls to monitor the growing number of ethnic minorities that congregate in ghettos in inner cities, and make these places no-go areas for other social groups.

Then the governments can *blame* faith schools that foster and bolster social division by restricting their intake to those of a particular faith. Of course, the justice system can sort things out once and for all, and find the *blameworthy* guilty. But who is to *blame* for the fact that the custodial sentence will be in a place which is a veritable breeding ground for lifelong criminals?

The blame game is a long game. There are as many answers to the question 'Who is to blame?' as there are observations about 'What's gone wrong'. So much wrong; so many to blame.

The Bible also has an answer to the question, 'What is wrong with the world?' Looking beneath the surface of presenting symptoms to the underlying causes, it says that the heart of the human problem is the problem of the human heart.[2] There was once a correspondence in a national newspaper under the heading 'What's wrong with the world?' I understand many contributors made a great variety of contributions, but none as succinct or searching as the man who wrote to the editor of the newspaper simply, 'I am' and signed off, 'Sincerely yours, G. K. Chesterton'.[3]

The Bible's verdict is not that the fault is all 'out there' with him, with her or with them. Nor does it concede that the problem is 'up there', as though the great creator was also a great wrecker. Rather, the Bible tells us that the fault lies 'in here', within each of us. Many of us may desire to be part of the solution to the problems of our world. But none of us can entirely escape the charge that we are part of the problem. We may want to be part of saving our world. But we, too, are part of the world of wrong that needs saving and changing.

In the letter that the apostle Paul wrote to Christians in Rome in the first century, he spoke about the good news that is at the heart of the Christian faith. 'I am not ashamed of the gospel,' he writes, 'because it is the power of God for the salvation of everyone who believes: first for the Jew, then for the Gentile' (Rom. 1:16).[4] But long before he explains much about the good news or gospel, which is the power of God for salvation, he writes at great length about the condition of the human race and its universal need for salvation.

---

2   I don't know the original source of this aphorism. Albert Einstein was close in saying 'The release of atom power has changed everything except our way of thinking... the solution to this problem lies in the heart of mankind. If only I had known, I should have become a watchmaker.'

3   Contribution to *The Times* newspaper topic 'What's wrong with the world', in 1908.

4   Unless otherwise indicated, inset Scripture quotes are taken from Romans in this chapter.

[18]The wrath of God is being revealed from heaven against all the godlessness and wickedness of men who suppress the truth by their wickedness, [19]since what may be known about God is plain to them, because God has made it plain to them. [20]For since the creation of the world God's invisible qualities – his eternal power and divine nature – have been clearly seen, being understood from what has been made, so that men are without excuse.

[21]For although they knew God, they neither glorified him as God nor gave thanks to him, but their thinking became futile and their foolish hearts were darkened. [22]Although they claimed to be wise, they became fools [23]and exchanged the glory of the immortal God for images made to look like mortal man and birds and animals and reptiles.

[24]Therefore God gave them over in the sinful desires of their hearts to sexual impurity for the degrading of their bodies with one another. [25]They exchanged the truth of God for a lie, and worshipped and served created things rather than the Creator – who is forever praised. Amen.

[26]Because of this, God gave them over to shameful lusts. Even their women exchanged natural relations for unnatural ones. [27]In the same way the men also abandoned natural relations with women and were inflamed with lust for one another. Men committed indecent acts with other men, and received in themselves the due penalty for their perversion.

[28]Furthermore, since they did not think it worthwhile to retain the knowledge of God, he gave them over to a depraved mind, to do what ought not to be done. [29]They have become filled with every kind of wickedness, evil, greed and depravity. They are full of envy, murder, strife, deceit and malice. They are gossips, [30]slanderers, God-haters, insolent, arrogant and

boastful; they invent ways of doing evil; they disobey their parents; [31]they are senseless, faithless, heartless, ruthless. [32]Although they know God's righteous decree that those who do such things deserve death, they not only continue to do these very things but also approve of those who practise them. (1:18-32)

A REJECTION OF GOD

It was to this passage that the nineteenth-century preacher, C.H.Spurgeon, applied the description 'the most painful of inspired scriptures'. If it is painful, it is because the truth hurts. What, according to this passage, is the truth about the human condition?

The essential charge is that human nature characteristically suppresses the truth about God. Whether we *say* there is no God or whether, more commonly, we simply *live* without reference to God, the charge here is that this attitude is born of a wilful and wicked determination to suppress the truth that God has made plain to all:

> [19]since what may be known about God is *plain* to them, because God has made it *plain* to them. [20]For since the creation of the world God's invisible qualities – his eternal power and divine nature – have been *clearly seen*, being understood from what has been made, so that men are *without excuse*. (1:19-20; emphasis added)

Of course, many say that they do not believe in God. But the Bible's own explanation for this is not that God is hiding but that we are. God has not concealed the evidence for his existence ('what may be known about God is *plain*....God has made it *plain*'). But we have a vested interest in suppressing the truth about God, or hiding away from his gaze. It suits us, who know full well about God, to suppress the truth about him because by so doing we are freed up from having to live for him, or as the writer here says 'to thank him or glorify him':

> For although they knew God, they neither glorified him as God nor gave thanks to him... . (1:21)

Those who choose to live the Christian life find that an appetite to know God is much reduced when we have a desire to do things of which we think God would not approve, or when we are running away from responsibilities we think he is laying on us.

It takes only a little self-awareness to know that the prospect of doing away with any figure of authority in our lives holds out the hope that we will be free. To live an unfettered life, free of external constraints both moral and spiritual, is instinctively attractive. The child often wants to be free of a parent's authority, as also a pupil of a teacher's authority. A motorist in a hurry will hope the cops aren't out and that the cameras are off. A slack and half-hearted worker is likely to fear and resent an employer's authority. And ultimately a rebellious or treacherous citizen despises a king's authority.

So, too, in the spiritual realm, whatever the risks – and these are real – we can easily echo the sentiment expressed by one writer '...remember, I had always wanted, above all things, not to be "interfered with". I had wanted (mad wish) "to call my soul my own"'. He sought to avoid God, and any claim God may make on his life, saying he felt 'the steady, unrelenting approach of him whom I so earnestly desired not to meet'. God was for him, a 'transcendental interferer' – from whom he wanted to be free.[5]

Jesus both assumed this truth about human nature and taught it. He told a story, for example, about a father (representing God) and his sons (representing God's people). It begins:

---

5   Quotations from *Surprised by Joy*, by C.S. Lewis (p. 182).

> 'There was a man who had two sons,' he said. [12]'The younger one said to his father, "Father, give me my share of the estate." So he divided his property between them. [13]Not long after that, the younger son got together all he had, set off for a distant country and there squandered his wealth in wild living.' (Luke 15:11b-13)

All this is but the background to all that the apostle Paul goes on to say in the passage quoted earlier about why the world is as it is. Our rejection *of* God, in our thinking and living, leads to a rejection *by* God. It is as though God says to a world that wants to live without him, 'If you insist on being on your own, on your own you will be'.

But getting what we think we want is not the blessing we imagine it will be. If, as the proverb goes, a person gets given enough rope (=freedom) to 'go and hang himself', the person's freedom is a recipe for their destruction. And a rejection *of* God that leads to a rejection *by* God is indeed full of fearsome consequences.

These consequences are now spelled out. Three times in this passage from the apostle Paul's letter we now read of what follows when God gives us up to ourselves and our perverse desire for 'freedom' from himself. Each is an expression of God's present wrath – or just judgment – on mankind's rebellion against God.

SPIRITUAL IDOLATRY

First, God gives us up to spiritual idolatry. A rejection of the truth about the creator God does not necessarily lead to the abandonment of all attempts to construct a religious view of reality. On the contrary, perhaps most common among those who have abandoned their conviction about a creator God, to which creation and the Bible testify, is their faith in some sort of 'higher power'. So the apostle Paul says,

> Although they claimed to be wise, they became fools
> and exchanged the glory of the immortal God for
> images made to look like mortal man and birds and
> animals and reptiles. (1:23)

Here is a description of crude idolatry. As we saw earlier,
we may think our own God-substitutes are of a different
order of sophistication from those of other times and
cultures. But whatever our idols, the underlying reality
is the same. The truth of God is being suppressed; the
God-substitute is being served.

And now for the real shock. When a world turns from
God in this way, God himself, in his wrath, *gives us up* to our
sinful desires – especially here of our minds. The exchange
of the 'glory of the immortal God for images made to look
like mortal man', which was something of our choosing,
becomes the essence of God's just judgment, as that
exchange becomes ever more deeply embedded in us:

> Therefore God gave them over ... They exchanged
> the truth of God for a lie, and worshipped and served
> created things rather than the Creator ... (1:25)

What we would never know if we didn't here have God's
Word to tell us is that suppression of the truth about God
leads in turn to spiritual blindness. The truth about God
that I *won't* see becomes the truth about God that I *can't*
see. As our writer also says, '...their *thinking* became futile
and their foolish *hearts* were darkened'. The reference here
to 'hearts' being darkened is not to the heart as that part
of us that 'feels' (in contrast to the mind being that part
of us that thinks). Rather, in the Bible, the heart is the
centre of the whole personality, and includes the mind,
will and emotions. A darkened heart is then, in the fullest
sense, a life without spiritual light and sight.

So, idolatry, in all its forms, is both a choice we make,
and a judgment God passes on us. No wonder that our

world is beset by a bewildering array of spiritual thought forms, very many of them utterly contradictory. In the Western world in our own day, only one absolute is all but universally admired, and that is that all spiritual points of view are equally valid, and to be tolerated as such. Politically, this way of thinking is attractive because it argues for the protection of people from the tyranny of 'thought police' and from any one religious grouping seeking to assert itself by force or force of law over others. The First Amendment to the American Constitution, ratified in 1791, states 'Congress shall make no law respecting an establishment of religion, or prohibiting the free exercise thereof...'.

But spiritually, it is nonsense. The plain truth is that it suits us to reject the plain truth about the creator God and to behave as though we are free of him. But, according to the apostle, this way of life then brings with it God's judgment so that those who *will not* know him find that they *cannot* see him.

MORAL CONFUSION

A rejection of God leads, secondly, to God giving us up to moral waywardness. A world which has refused to know God is a world which God has been prepared to give over to 'shameful lusts'.

> [26]Because of this, God gave them over to shameful lusts. Even their women exchanged natural relations for unnatural ones. [27]In the same way the men also abandoned natural relations with women and were inflamed with lust for one another. Men committed indecent acts with other men, and received in themselves the due penalty for their perversion. (1:26-27)

Few areas of modern life are as controversial as sexual ethics. In a liberal Western democracy what consenting adults do in private is beyond the law to control, and beyond public opinion to censure. Therefore, it is inevitable that in the minds of many it is the Bible – or a literal interpretation of it – that is, once again, called into question. But if, as we're assuming in this investigation of the Christian faith, the Bible provides the gold standard, the benchmark, of what is godly and true, then this controversy cannot be avoided.

The truth presented here is that it is not a glorious thing for two women, or indeed two men, to engage in sexual relations. It is – or ought to be – a matter of shame. And our same-sex desires, along with the fantasy of all manner of heterosexual fulfilment outside our committed marriage relationships, are not the full and beautiful flowering of our humanity, but the judgment of God on rebellious humanity. It is because mankind has refused to acknowledge God as its maker that he has given us over to the shameful lusts that we all experience.

Once again we are seeing that the choices we make, here described as 'the exchange' we make, carry only the illusion of a free choice made with a noble mind. Underneath what presents itself as 'going where love leads' is the reality of our inclination to abandon right ways of thinking and living, and – worse – the reality of God abandoning us and giving us up to ourselves and our perverse inclinations.

Of course, the sexual appetite and instinct is often so strong that no petty moralizing from the statute book of a parliament or the pulpit of a local church can have much effect. Whether our sexual fantasies play themselves out in lustful looks and adulterous acts with the opposite sex or we are 'inflamed with lust for one another', to a greater or lesser degree many, if not all of us, are – or have been – out of control in this area.

But the issue is more serious than that because, once again, it is not simply that we *do not* think straight, but that we *cannot*. 'Men committed indecent acts with other men, and received in themselves the due penalty for their perversion' (v. 27). What is the 'penalty for the perversion'? Not, surely, as some have claimed, AIDS; this is recent, and cannot have been in the apostle's mind as he wrote. Much more likely the 'penalty' is a mindset which *approves* of the practice. So, too, God's judgment on mankind that is determined to reject his standards will, in part, be experienced in mankind approving different standards of its own making. Says our writer:

> Although they know God's righteous decree that those who do such things deserve death, they not only continue to do these very things but also approve of those who practise them. (1:32, and see below)

SOCIAL DISINTEGRATION

We are sexual beings, with strong sexual preferences, and all that adds fire and fury to any discussion of sexual ethics. I do understand that many who stumble across the preceding paragraphs will struggle to read further without deep suspicion. But what is controversial in our day is not all-consuming for the apostle as he presses on with his theme of what abandonment by God looks like in practice in our lives today.

He adds to the categories of spiritual idolatry and moral confusion a further sign of God giving us up to ourselves – social disintegration. He identifies a catalogue of sins which are not essentially spiritual or sexual but social – in the sense that they destroy relationships. We read here of

> envy, murder, strife, deceit and malice. They are gossips, [30]slanderers, God-haters, insolent, arrogant and boastful; they invent ways of doing evil; they disobey their parents; [31]they are senseless, faithless, heartless and ruthless. (1:29b-31)

None of this is headline-grabbing news. It is all far too common to be newsworthy; too familiar to be intriguing. It's just the way we are in our world. If there was any danger from the earlier paragraphs of any one of us saying 'I'm not like that', we now find we are fairly and squarely caught up in the categories of sin which mean we also are among those who have been given up by God to ourselves.

Once again, however, the position is worse than it seems. Because if a person could come to terms with their sin, for example, the sin of being 'boastful', then it is conceivable that that person might try to change his boastful way of thinking and speaking about himself. But the problem is with recognizing sin *as sin;* the problem is not primarily with behaviour but with the mind:

> [28]Furthermore, since they did not think it worthwhile to retain the knowledge of God, he gave them over to a depraved mind, to do what ought not to be done.

> [32]Although they know God's righteous decree that those who do such things deserve death, they not only continue to do these very things but also approve of those who practise them. (1:28, 32)

The consequence of our refusal to know God is that God gives us over to 'a depraved mind'. The mind no longer functions, as God intended, to be a moral compass and to give direction as it should. The evidence of a depraved mind is not only to be found in practising sin, but in approving it; not so much in breaking God's laws as presuming to make our own.

So, to take an example from the apostle's list of social sins, there is no moral or spiritual distinction between (a) being a 'gossip' (b) publishing it in a newspaper article or (c) rushing out to buy the paper to gloat over it at home. Or again, there is no distinction of spiritual significance between being immoral and approving of immorality. It is a case of, 'You are not what you think you are, but what "you think", you are.' The problem is not just with the way we live, but the way we think. And that is not something we can change at will. It is the judgment of God in the present on the lives of those who choose to reject the truth about God.

Here is the reason why neither exhortation – addressed to the will – nor education – addressed to the mind – can significantly change human behaviour. To know real lasting change in my behaviour, I need a miracle. I need a new heart and a renewed mind if I am to live a life that is pleasing to God. I need God to save me.

A RIGHTEOUS CRITIC

One reason why, instinctively, many of us draw back from this appraisal of the human condition is that it is so uncompromisingly dark. It seems to make no allowance for the good in many a human heart, or for the clear distinctions between the good and the bad in society. A self-respecting person may say, 'I am not as bad as you say I am, and I am certainly not as bad as (some) others.' This attitude resonates with us. Indeed, a modicum of self-respect seems to demand that we do not simply say, 'I'm all bad.' If what Christians believe seems to demand the condemnation of the whole human race, so much the worse for what Christians believe.

The hidden assumption, or hope at least for many of us, is that I am good enough in God's sight. And this hope that I am good enough for God, and not as bad as others, finds its expression in a judgmental spirit, putting others down. It is an attitude to which the writer of this letter, to the Christians in Rome, now turns his attention:

> You, therefore, have no excuse, you who pass judgment on someone else, for at whatever point you judge the other, you are condemning yourself, because you who pass judgment do the same things. (2:1)

It seems to many of us there is a spectrum of good and evil, and whether consciously or subconsciously, we are continually placing ourselves and others somewhere on that spectrum. I may put myself rather below others, an attitude we commonly identify with low self-esteem which constantly says 'I am not as good as her'. Or we may put ourselves rather above others, like the fictional character in one of Jesus' stories:

> 'God, I thank you that I am not like other men – robbers, evildoers, adulterers... [12]I fast twice a week and give a tenth of all I get.' (Luke 18:11b-12)

It is this latter self-righteous attitude which is the real ground of hope for many of us. I say in my heart, if not with my lips, 'Thank you God that I am not like other people. I do not do the wrong they do. And I do the good they do not do.' However, this attempt at self-justification, by making flattering comparisons of myself with others, is doomed to failure. The writer gives two reasons. First,

> 'You, therefore, have no excuse, you who pass judgment on someone else, for at whatever point you judge the other, you are condemning yourself, because you who pass judgment do the same things.' (2:1)

We are prone to judge. But, the point is, we are especially prone to do so when we find someone else doing the very thing that we recognise to be wrong in our own hearts and lives. I can spot gossip in another, because I have so often been a gossip myself. I can sniff out greed in another, because I can recognise in my own heart the craving for more. I am alert to deceitfulness in others, because I know the temptation to be economical with the truth.

Yes, the sins I observe in others, and for which I judge others, are invariably the sins with which I am most familiar in my own heart, even if they manifest themselves differently in my life. And therefore in making what might be a right judgment of someone else, I am invariably condemning myself because 'I do the same things.' As Jesus famously said to the accusers of a woman caught in adultery, 'If any one of you is without sin, let him be the first to throw a stone at her' (John 8:7). Needless to say, no stones were thrown.

There is a second reason why judging others, which is so natural to us, is so fatal. It is because passing judgment on others gives us the illusion of being safe from judgment ourselves. There is nothing like playing the judge to give us hope that we shall escape the judgment. But the hope is futile; he goes on to say:

> So when you, a mere man, pass judgment on them and yet do the same things, do you think you will escape God's judgment? (2:3)

There is no escape from God's judgment for 'mere man', not even where he plays the part that properly, and ultimately, belongs to God himself. To judge others may make us feel safe, because it makes us feel superior, but it is not possible to put ourselves above the judgment, not even by playing the part of the judge.

We remain mere mortal men and women, liable to the judgment of God. And the sharpness of our evaluation and judgment of others, far from being a sign of superiority and safety, is in reality only a nail in the coffin of our own fatal self-righteousness.

Even now, God could bring his judgment on us in full and final measure. We are not to construe God's withholding of that full judgment right now as a sign that he will not judge us in the future. On the contrary, God's delayed judgment is an opportunity given to us by God, in his kindness, tolerance and patience, to turn from wrong and seek from God the mercy we so badly need[6].

But self-righteousness is a most stubborn illusion. There is nothing quite like it. Our consciences ought to be cringing at our own failure; but instead they are accusing someone else. We ought to be cowering before the judge of all the earth; instead we are presuming to do his work, and execute his judgment on the world. Our own high moral standards ought to be making us fearful; instead, they make us feel fearlessly superior. We scoff at the prospect of judgment, fondly imagining God will give us what we have earned and deserved – little realizing how much our own self-righteousness blinds us to our true natures and the deservedness of a just and awful judgment.

And worse is to come. Our fatal self-righteousness has an ally in religion.

REFUGE IN RELIGION

In our own age, and in Western Europe in particular, a formal commitment to a faith, and to public worship, is not as widespread as it has been in the past. Nevertheless, it still evokes in the eyes of many non-participants a sense of admiration. Religious groups and faith communities may get tacit support from the state through their charitable status, and recognition by local councils. People commonly assume faith groups are essentially good people advancing the cause of public-spirited, decent community living.

And this is how we who are religious people often see ourselves. Is it not an easy thing for the synagogue, church or mosque attendee to be saying, in his heart, 'I am a good

---

6   'Or do you show contempt for the riches of his kindness, tolerance and patience, not realising that God's kindness leads you towards repentance?' (Rom. 2:4).

'The Lord is not slow in keeping his promise, as some understand slowness. He is patient with you, not wanting anyone to perish, but everyone to come to repentance' (2 Pet. 3:9).

man'? Religion can quickly become, in the eyes of those who espouse its tenets and practise its requirements, a seal of good citizenship and a badge of good behaviour.

But, once again, the danger is that I believe I have attained personally to the image I present of myself publicly. I allow the best of my public image to be the right measure of the real inner me. The high standards I espouse are suggestive of a very good life and, unthinkingly, I begin to imagine that in the same way I have loved the teaching, I have actually lived the life. It's a terrible confusion. The writer to the church in Rome exposes the error, and applies his insight in the first instance to the religious Jew:

> [17]Now you, if you call yourself a Jew; if you rely on the law and brag about your relationship to God; [18]if you know his will and approve of what is superior because you are instructed by the law; [19]if you are convinced that you are a guide for the blind, a light for those who are in the dark, [20]an instructor of the foolish, a teacher of infants, because you have in the law the embodiment of knowledge and truth – [21]you, then, who teach others, do you not teach yourself? You who preach against stealing, do you steal? [22]You who say that people should not commit adultery, do you commit adultery? You who abhor idols, do you rob temples? [23]You who brag about the law, do you dishonour God by breaking the law? [24]As it is written: 'God's name is blasphemed among the Gentiles because of you'. (2:17-24)

This was written to those whose religious background was Jewish. But it would apply more widely to those whose religious affiliation is similarly indicative of high moral and social ideals. There are two great risks attaching to the practice of such a religion.

The first – but lesser risk – is the risk of deceiving the public. Notwithstanding my faith may be practised privately, it invariably makes a public statement. It says not only, 'this is the teaching I believe,' but inevitably also the corollary, 'this is the teaching I follow.' And yet, to a greater or lesser degree, this will be found to be false.

There will be a chasm between my private ideals and my public standards, and sooner or later the world discovers that. Sometimes this takes the form of a particularly public scandal. A religious leader of some note has had his hands in the till or the wrong someone in his bed or there is a blatant deception about his ministry. But more common, and more prosaic, is the multitude of lesser names in which the world recognises a discrepancy between the faith that is professed and the life that is lived. There is more than a whiff of hypocrisy in the air, as those who teach and profess to live by one standard actually live by another. It is a deception and a way of life which both dishonours God, and causes the world looking on to dishonour the God in whose name such hypocrisy is practised: 'As it is written: "God's name is blasphemed among the Gentiles because of you"' (Rom. 2:24).

But there is a second and – for our present purposes – greater risk attached to the practice of religion which is that it not only deceives the world, but it also deceives the worshipper. If self-righteousness is a peculiarly impenetrable darkness surrounding the human soul, the practice of religion makes it doubly so. It not only lends weight to my own self-perception that I am good, but it will tend to make me feel safe.

In belonging to the supportive faith community of church, synagogue, temple or mosque, I shall no doubt find I am accepted, perhaps even applauded for my way of life. Closing ranks against the world of 'unbelievers' outside I shall perhaps be even less liable to come to terms with a truthful assessment of my life, namely that my life falls a very long way short of the high ideals and lofty standards of my sacred book.

This taking refuge in religion to make me feel safe with God would be sensible if the refuge was indeed secure. But religion, as a refuge against the inevitable judgment of God who sees the heart, is worthless.

> The Lord does not look at the things man looks at. Man looks at the outward appearance, but the Lord looks at the heart. (1 Sam. 16:7)

Although an outward conformity to a moral and religious code will gain me earthly friends and the praise of the spiritual leadership or human priesthood to whom I give account now, it will ultimately do nothing to make me right with the God to whom I am finally and completely accountable on the judgment day to come. Religion is, therefore, very dangerous; it can calm lurking fears and numb an uneasy conscience. The writer of this letter to the church in Rome knew that; he was zealously religious as only few know how to be.[7] And yet, speaking to his fellow Jews, he writes:

> Circumcision has value if you observe the law, but if you break the law, you have become as though you had not been circumcised. (2:25)

In other words, the practice of religion (in this case, the Jewish faith, characterised by circumcision – a symbol of submission to the Jewish law) is valueless without a life which does, in fact, keep God's law perfectly. And as we have seen, no-one does keep God's law perfectly.

---

7   Paul writes elsewhere of his impeccable religious pedigree: 'If anyone else thinks he has reasons to put confidence in the flesh, I have more: circumcised on the eighth day, of the people of Israel, of the tribe of Benjamin, a Hebrew of Hebrews; in regard to the law a Pharisee; as for zeal, persecuting the church; as for legalistic righteousness, faultless'. Philippians 3:4-6

So, being a Jew does not make me safe. Indeed religion – of any sort – is no place of safety for sinful men and women. And one shocking way of exposing the religiously self-righteous Jew to the terrible implications of this truth is to say, as the writer here does, that a non-Jew, obeying God's law, would be in a position to condemn the law-breaking Jew:

> The one who is not circumcised physically and yet obeys the law will condemn you who, even though you have the written code and circumcision, are a law-breaker[8]. (2:27)

Religion is simply not the refuge that we who are religious make it out to be. And the reason is not hard to find; indeed, it is usually obvious, at least to the irreligious who care to give this any thought. It is that religion is almost exclusively concerned with externals. Tampering with what lies on the outside of man, religious observance of this ritual or that ceremony, does nothing to change a man on the inside. The practice of religion may make me an insider with others who are similarly persuaded; indeed the praise of men can be what makes the practice of religion so appealing.[9] But, because religion doesn't change my heart, it wins me no favours with God. As we've seen, I need, amongst other things, a heart change that religion is powerless to supply:

> [28]A man is not a Jew if he is only one outwardly, nor is circumcision merely outward and physical. [29]No, a man is a Jew if he is one inwardly; and circumcision

---

8 Paul's language here is not to point the way to salvation (see the next chapter), but to show Jews that their position is essentially no different from that of the Gentiles.

9 Jesus said 'How can you believe if you accept praise from one another, yet make no effort to obtain the praise that comes from the only God?' John 5:44.

is circumcision of the heart, by the Spirit, not by the written code. Such a man's praise is not from men, but from God. (2:28-29)

So we are back where we started; the heart of the human problem is the problem of the human heart. The human heart – yours and mine – is spiritually corrupt; we do not honour God as God. And the human heart is morally wayward; we do not love others as we ought. And neither the religiously zealous nor the morally superior have a place of safety, much as we often think otherwise. What the Jewish Scriptures say to the Jewish people, the Jewish Scriptures say to us all. None can escape the charge which God brings against us:

> There is no-one righteous, not even one;
> [11]There is no-one who understands, no-one who seeks God.
> [12]All have turned away, they have together become worthless;
> there is no-one who does good, not even one.
> [13]Their throats are open graves; their tongues practise deceit.
> The poison of vipers is on their lips.
> [14]Their mouths are full of cursing and bitterness.
> [15]Their feet are swift to shed blood;
> [16]ruin and misery mark their ways,
> [17]and the way of peace they do not know.
> [18]There is no fear of God before their eyes.
> (3:10b-18, quoting a number of Jewish Scriptures)

'No-one is good'. Quoting what the Jewish Scriptures (the Christian Old Testament) say about the Jewish nation, this is the oft-repeated thought. *No-one* is good. 'There is *no-one* righteous, *not even one;* there is *no-one* who understands, *no-one* who seeks God. *All* have turned away, they have *together* become worthless; there is *no-one* who does good, *not even one*' (Rom. 3:10-12). The writer concludes:

> Now we know that whatever the law says, it says to those who are under the law, so that every mouth may be silenced and the whole world held accountable to God (3:19).

And again, a few verses later on, we will read

> There is no difference, for all have sinned and fall short of the glory of God... (3:23)

Why this emphasis on the *whole* human race? It is because of the age-old issue of human pride, which means that so many of us will secretly be hoping we are a cut above others, and that the indictment of the human race somehow doesn't include me.

Specifically, in the context, the writer is addressing Jewish pride. 'What shall we [i.e. we Jews] conclude then? Are we any better?' The answer he gives at every point, and here as he answers his own rhetorical question, is 'Not at all! We have already made the charge that Jews and Gentiles alike are all under sin' (Rom. 3:9).

It matters little, however, whether the source of human pride and the hope of escaping the condemnation of the human race spring from racial identity, religious affiliation, social class, personal morality, the praise of others or any intellectual or other achievement. On this issue of our standing before God, there is no real distinction between us, and that includes me, the writer, and every reader – and non-reader – of this book. It means we are *all* guilty before God, as charged. *No-one* is good.

The fact is that I am in the same boat as all mankind. Christians, as others, have a way of preaching, speaking and writing which appears to condemn some whilst exonerating others. This spiritual or moral one-upmanship is understandable; we are moral creatures making moral judgments. But in the larger scheme of events it is inexcusable, because we are all in the same boat. We are *all* moral bankrupts. We are *all* spiritual reprobates. No-one is good. And such distinctions as exist between us do *not* put us in different categories in God's eyes.

I return briefly to the graffiti artist who in answer to one piece of graffiti, 'Jesus is the answer', scribbled another asking, 'What's the question?' We need a truthful assessment of the state of the world and of the human condition before evaluating the multitude of remedies (social, political and religious) offered to meet it. We cannot know whether Jesus – or some other – is 'the answer' unless we know what the question is. What, then, has gone wrong with the world, and how can we summarise our human spiritual predicament?

The answer, in brief, is that we have turned away from God, and he in consequence has turned aside from us. We stand under God's wrath – that is, the deserved and just judgment of God. And that judgment cannot be cancelled without God's justice being called into question. If he doesn't judge, can he be just? That fearful and just wrath of God will be made manifest to our world in two ways.

First, in the present, God's wrath is experienced as he gives us up to ourselves – to spiritual idolatry, moral confusion, and social disharmony and disintegration. The ruined relationship between sinners and a perfect God is what needs to be restored, if the lifestyle that accompanies our God-forsakenness is to be changed.

Second, God's wrath will be manifest in the future. Those who persist in rebellion against God need to know, says the apostle Paul, that

> ...you are storing up wrath against yourself for the day of God's wrath, when his righteous judgment will be revealed. (2:5)

So, according to this letter from the apostle, what's gone wrong with the world is that we have turned from God, and we now stand under his wrath – his just judgment – both in the present ('the wrath of God is being revealed...') and the future ('the day of God's wrath...' Rom. 1:18; 2:5).

It may be tempting to think that the sense of crisis is overdone; that the scrape we have got ourselves into is a scrape we can get ourselves out of. Surely, we say, the things I have done wrong today I can put right tomorrow. With a word of apology, I can be reconciled to the people I have offended, and with an appropriate gesture I can make restitution to those I have robbed. This might be a fine start for a school's golden rules or a citizen's national charter, if our only need was to be reconciled to one another. But the Scriptures are saying our primary need is to be reconciled to God, from whom we have turned away. 'There is... no-one who *seeks God*. All have *turned away*' (that is, from God).

And the plain message we have been looking at is that there is no human bridge back to God. Perhaps this is obvious, but the writer Paul knew it needed saying to his Jewish readers, and doubtless it needs saying to a non-Jewish (as well as Jewish) audience today too.

For Jews had God's law; was that not a ladder to heaven for the law-abiding? And much of the world of our day has all the ethical teaching of the Old Testament (for example, the Ten Commandments) as well as Jesus' teaching in the New Testament (for example, the Sermon on the Mount). Is that not a ladder to heaven for those who do their best to love their neighbour and live a good life? We often feel so.

Is not the implicit hope at the funeral services of a multitude of men and women, and in the eulogies we hear of good characters and selfless deeds, that these were good people? In our hearts we say of a man we knew, 'He lived by God's law; he lived by his own light. That will surely be enough to bridge the gulf to God and to glory, to get him up the ladder to heaven's gate, and entry through heaven's door.'

This hope is widespread but our writer is clear that it is wrong. According to our writer, the law God has given to his people does not serve to acquit us; it condemns us. God's law is not a ladder to heaven, which we climb as we obey its precepts. Instead, God's law is a mirror into which we look and which shows us how far short we have fallen.

> Therefore no-one will be declared righteous in his sight by observing the law; rather, through the law we become conscious of sin. (3:20)

****

I suppose this has been a particularly depressing chapter to read, just as it has been to write! But two factors would make the bitter pill of its message easier to swallow.

The first factor is that human sinfulness provides an explanation for what's gone wrong with the world without us having to resort to the endless and futile 'blame game' or to the atheist's premise that there is no God and therefore no reason to believe this world could be better than it is.

Understandably, sensitive individuals are appalled and perplexed by human suffering. Face-to-face with the terrible suffering that afflicts the human race, atheism is *a* way through. It would go some way to explaining the pain and suffering of human existence. It gives its explanation of human suffering by saying there is no meaning or purpose behind human existence, and no reasonable expectation that life might be any different from the way it is. Of course, for some, that explanation will *add* considerably to the pain and suffering.

But more common than outright atheism is a practical atheism[10] – living as if there were no God – which, as we have been seeing, is how we are prone to live. And this observation concerning the deliberate suppression of the truth about God, humbling though it is to accept, shows that there is another explanation for the way things are. In refusing to honour God as God, he has given us up to ourselves, and we in turn are reaping the consequences – untold human misery caused by plain human sinfulness.

Alongside our daily neglect of the creator God, some cherish the vain hope that he will one day be in the dock and called to account for crimes against humanity. But we should not lose sight of our creaturely status. Living as though there were no God, whilst simultaneously imagining there is a good case against God, is a perilous position to be in. Far from God being in the dock, he will soon be on the bench as the all-seeing judge, bringing about a just outcome to all that blights our world. Then it will be clear, if never before, that the heart of the human problem was always the problem of the human heart:

> [29]They have become filled with every kind of wickedness, evil, greed and depravity. They are full of envy, murder, strife, deceit and malice. They are gossips, [30]slanderers, God-haters, insolent, arrogant and boastful; they invent ways of doing evil; they disobey their parents; [31]they are senseless, faithless, heartless, ruthless. (1:29-31)

There is a second factor which makes the bitter pill of human sinfulness easier to swallow. It is that – wonderfully – there *is* a solution. Just as many of us

---

10   See, for example, John Humphrys' *In God we Doubt*, which he subtitles 'Confessions of a Failed Atheist'.

will struggle to take on board the bad news of a serious illness if the sad reality is there is no known cure – being more inclined to bury our heads in the sand – so also without the very good news of a 'cure' for our ills, few of us would ever come to terms with the state of our hearts and lives before God.

For most of us it is the news of a rescue that enables us to come to terms with the fact of our rebellion against God that makes us deserving of his wrath. You, the reader, may be one such person who awaits the news of the next chapter before being able to take to heart the message of this present one. That has certainly been the case for me.

In answer to the question 'Does God care about the world that has gone so badly wrong?' the resounding answer is 'Yes!' – he cares deeply and has shown his care clearly and unmistakably by providing a solution so radical and personal that we cannot but sit up and take notice.

The essence of our need is someone to do for us what we cannot do for ourselves, which is bring us back to God. We need someone who will act on our behalf, and who can speak to God for us in our defence. We need a mediator with God. And the shape of such a needful mediator begins to be clear. He needs to be human, and able to act on our behalf, and divine so that he can act for God. The good news of the Christian faith, explored in the next chapter, is that there is just such a mediator as we need!

> [5]For there is one God and one mediator between God and men, the man Christ Jesus, [6]who gave himself as a ransom for all men... . (1 Tim. 2:5-6)

Does God care?

One thing at least can be said with certainty about the crucifixion of Christ. It was manifestly the most famous death in history.

MALCOLM MUGGERIDGE

For me, the turning point in caring about what Christians believe was discovering that they have some very good news to tell – what one writer succinctly, and without exaggeration, called 'the best news in the world'. At the time, it felt like stumbling across treasure quite unexpectedly.

Perhaps I had heard it a thousand times before, but it had made no impression upon me. Why not? What has the power to make the very best news seem as drab as a rainy day, or as inconsequential as an unchanging tax code from Her Majesty's Revenue and Customs?

I think three things stood in the way of my hearing this good news as good news. First, it was made to seem complicated. I recall on one occasion attending a discussion group at a church, but was unable to contribute anything to the discussion. At the close, the group leader asked if I, or another silent member, would like to say anything, and I replied along the lines of 'Yes, I would like to say something. I haven't understood a word anyone has said all evening!' I am sure I was blind and deaf to many insightful comments but, in part, the issues were made too complicated.

Second, the message was encrusted. It was overlaid with too much stuff. Some who reject Christian teaching are actually rejecting the garb that it gets clothed with: old and often cold buildings, mournful music and large amounts of liturgy, unnatural-sounding voices and the routine of sombre services. It would help if much of this encrustation could be scraped away, but the impression can be given that it is essential, and that's what really does the damage. Certainly for me, at that time, the message was inseparable from all the external stuff that clothed it – as I felt – so unattractively.

Third, and perhaps more significantly, I had a limited appetite for spiritual truth. As we have seen in the last chapter, it suited me well enough to get by without God, if I could. The old adage that you can take a horse to water, but you cannot make it drink is true in the spiritual realm too. To change the analogy, there are none as blind as those that will not see. And I had no real sense of need to which the Christian faith on offer was any sort of an answer.

All this began to change for me for several reasons I can recall. First, I met with practising Christians who made Christian living a reality from which I could not escape. I knew I was not one of them. But I was seeing the Christian faith lived out in a compelling and contemporary way, and could no longer hide behind the excuse that the church was old-fashioned and irrelevant. In a way this was thrilling. Realistically, it was also threatening. In the end, however, it crystallised in me a desire to know the reality and to ditch the façade of the faith to which I had clung for some time as a more or less nominal churchgoer.

Second, subconsciously I was realizing that life was more about people than about things; strength to love people, therefore, was a primary need, not a luxury item, and I needed that. In passing, someone had commented that Christianity was about 'strength to love' – the title of a book by Martin Luther King, the civil rights activist in America. That made Christianity seem relevant in a new way. I could not, of course, have articulated a doctrine of human sin such as we have looked at in the last chapter, nor did I know of the possibility of a 'new heart', or 'new birth.'[1] But in a small way I was becoming more aware of my innate selfishness, and already I could see I needed 'heart surgery'.

But third, and most importantly, I met with one man in particular who explained quite simply why Jesus died. This was the very good news I needed to hear. It took full account of the kind of person I was, and the kind of God he is, and showed how I could know him. What more could I have wanted?

MY TESTIMONY

Our memories can let us down and our imaginations can make up for the shortfall; we can both forget the truth and embellish it. But as best as I can recall, I made my way to a Christian friend's house one afternoon during my first year at Bristol University. He worked for the local church. He mentioned, more or less in passing, that he was about to give a talk about the meaning and significance of Jesus' death on a cross.

As he told me this, I recall that I was fascinated, because I really didn't know why Jesus died on the cross. But I was fearful of displaying my ignorance; perhaps after two decades of being in and out of church I should know and understand *something* of the significance of Jesus' death.

---

1   The prophet Ezekiel (36:26) famously records God's promise to his people, 'I will give you a new heart and put a new spirit in you; I will remove from you your heart of stone and give you a heart of flesh.' See further, chapter 7 below.

In fact, however, the fact of Jesus' death really meant nothing to me at all. I could recite the Apostles' Creed with the best of them – 'suffered under Pontius Pilate, was crucified, died and was buried; he descended to the dead'. But really, so what?

In the end, and although it meant admitting I understood very little, curiosity caused me to ask for an explanation. Why *did* Jesus die? My friend, David, explained with a verse from the Old Testament:

> We all, like sheep, have gone astray, each of us has turned to his own way, and the Lord has laid on him the iniquity of us all. (Isa. 53:6)

Perhaps he saw my eyes glaze over! Here were more words, but – as yet – no more insight. What helped was a simple visual aid. Putting one hand out, palm upwards, he placed a book on it. Imagine, he said, that the hand is you and that God is where the light on the ceiling is, and that this book resting on the hand is your sin. He went through the first part of the verse again.

> 'We all, like sheep, have gone astray, each of us has turned to his own way...'

The book resting on his hand was cutting that hand off from the source of light on the ceiling. And that, he explained, was what my sin was doing for me – cutting me off from God. Just as that book was a barrier that prevented the light shining on the hand, so my sin was a barrier that prevented God knowing me, and me knowing him, in any kind of personal relationship. This was something I didn't really want to hear.

But my friend pressed ahead with the verse. '...and the Lord has laid on him the iniquity of us all'. At this point David transferred the book resting on the one hand (representing me cut off from God) onto his other hand representing Jesus (when he died on the cross). And he explained that when Jesus died on the cross the Lord (God) was transferring my sin, and the judgment I deserved for it, *onto Jesus*.

As the book was transferred away from the hand that represented me, it was clear that the barrier between God and me was removed. And that struck me immediately. Here was the answer to how I could be brought to know God despite the fact I deserved to be cut off from him: it was all because, on the cross, Jesus bore the judgment that my sin deserved, so that God was able to see me, and treat me, as sinless.

Here was a great and glorious exchange; my sin taken by Jesus and laid to his account and, in exchange, his sinless life credited to my account.

This was not what some call a 'Damascus Road' experience – but as best as I can recall, this was the moment the penny dropped for me. Here was almost unbelievably good news. Here, wonderfully, I was learning how it was possible to have a relationship with God *despite* my total lack of deserving. Without me trying to fool God that I was better than I really was, I learnt that – thanks to the death of Jesus in my place – God was able to accept me, forgive me, know me and assure me that I would never be held to account for my sin. As a result of Jesus' death, God was able to deal with me not on the basis of the *judgment I deserved* but the *mercy Jesus secured*.

******

I have included this account of my story to show how truth came to life for me. But up until now I have wanted to resist telling 'my story'; I would rather explain *what*

Christians believe than give an account of my experience. That is because all that can be claimed for a personal experience is that some person claims to have had it; but where does that leave everyone else?

I quickly discovered, however, that my experience, far from being exceptional, was a thoroughly normal Christian experience. For the single verse of the Bible that my friend had used to such helpful effect in my life was all of a piece with the Bible's teaching more widely on this central issue of 'how can I be put right with God?'

We turn, then, to look at one clear explanation in the Bible of how through the death of Jesus we can be put right with God. But just before looking at the detail, we should see the big picture and know that the death of Jesus for us is the fundamental proof of God's care for a lost and broken world. The question which I have made the title for this chapter, 'Does God care?' is answered definitively and positively at the cross.

At the cross, God says to a lost world, 'I love you still.' Your finances are a mess? God says, 'I love you still.' Your family has disowned you? 'I love you still.' You have treated people badly, and they won't forget it? 'I love you still.' You have an addiction to drink or drugs? 'I love you still.' You are crushed by disappointed hopes and unfulfilled dreams? 'I love you still.' You feel guilty and ashamed and can't recover a clean conscience or a lost innocence? 'I love you still.' You have wandered a long way from God? He says... 'I love you still.' It's the central message of the Bible. Jesus himself says,

> 'I am the good shepherd. The good shepherd lays down his life for the sheep.' (John 10:11)

The apostle Peter says:

> For Christ died for sins once for all, the righteous for
> the unrighteous, to bring you to God. (1 Pet. 3:18)

The apostle Paul says:

> But God demonstrates his own love for us in this: while
> we were still sinners, Christ died for us. (Rom. 5:8)

So, also, does the apostle John:

> For God so loved the world that he gave his one and
> only Son, that whoever believes in him shall not perish
> but have eternal life. (John 3:16)

Therefore, we are on solid ground when we look to the death of Jesus on the cross as the supreme proof that God cares for a world that has gone wrong, and that he loves those who – as yet – are lost to him. It is never right to say, or imply, that God hates people of any race, class, sexual orientation or religion. 'For God so *loved* the world that he gave his one and only Son...'.

More magnificent still, however, God's love doesn't leave us in our ignorance and waywardness. On the contrary, God is powerful enough to rescue the wayward world which he loves, and restore it to himself.

The death of Jesus on the cross is both the definitive demonstration of the *love of God* and of the *power of God* to bring us to him.

HOW CAN WE BE PUT RIGHT WITH GOD?

We saw in the last chapter that we have all turned aside from God, and God in his righteous anger has turned aside from us. If that is indeed the case, the question we will long to have answered is 'how can we be established back in a right relationship with God?'

We are going to look at the answer that the apostle Paul goes on to give in the letter he wrote to the church in Rome that we began to look at in the last chapter.

In the passage that follows, the words which speak of us being in a right relationship with God are: 'righteous', 'righteousness' and 'justified'. To be declared 'righteous' in God's sight (or to be 'justified') is to be declared fit to stand before him, and to relate to him, without guilt or shame. Righteousness is therefore the quality of fitness for the presence of God that we all need. This is Paul explaining how we can have that 'righteousness' that we need:

> [20]Therefore no-one will be declared righteous in his sight by observing the law; rather through the law we become conscious of sin.
>
> [21]But now a righteousness from God, apart from law, has been made known, to which the Law and the prophets testify. [22]This righteousness from God comes through faith in Jesus Christ to all who believe. There is no difference, [23]for all have sinned and fall short of the glory of God, [24]and are justified freely by his grace through the redemption that came by Christ Jesus. [25]God presented him as a sacrifice of atonement through faith in his blood. He did this to demonstrate his justice, because in his forbearance he had left the sins committed beforehand unpunished – [26]he did it to demonstrate his justice at the present time, so as to be just and the one who justifies those who have faith in Jesus. (Rom. 3:20-26)

On first reading this will likely seem complicated but, believe me, it isn't. There are three truths being made crystal clear here concerning being made right with God and we will look at each. This righteousness, or right standing with God,

1. **comes to us 'apart from law...'**

2. **comes to us 'through the redemption that came by Christ Jesus'.**

3. **comes to us 'through faith in Christ Jesus'.**

1. This right standing with God comes to us 'apart from law...' (v. 21)

God has found a way to put us right with himself, and it has nothing to do with us keeping his law – which, as we have seen, is something we are powerless to do. Therefore, God's way of making us right with himself is *'apart from law'*:

> [20]Therefore no-one will be declared righteous in his sight by observing the law; rather through the law we become conscious of sin. [21]But now a righteousness from God, apart from law, has been made known, to which the Law and the prophets testify. (Rom. 3:20-21)

Note the contrast being drawn: 'no-one will be declared righteous in his sight *by observing the law...*' 'But now a righteousness from God, *apart from law*, has been made known...' (v. 21).

In this one contrast being drawn, we are very close to the heart of God's good news. It is that the perfectly good or righteous life that we are powerless to present to God because of our inability to keep God's law, is a righteous life which God will present, or credit, *to* us.

This right standing with God comes to us as a gift *from God*, and not as a result of our own doing. It is not something we can deserve or achieve; it is something that God gives which we can only receive. It is given *'freely by his grace'* (v. 24), the word 'grace' describing the character of God who generously gives to us what we do not deserve and what we cannot achieve for ourselves.

Not all of us are good at receiving gifts. Perhaps, especially, those who are characteristically family providers, breadwinners, 'self-made' achievers, present-givers or charity-supporters will struggle to see that we ourselves must come with empty hands and rely on God. We must receive from him what can only come as a gift from his hands. It is a shock for those who have – often rightly – been self-reliant in material terms to discover that self-reliance is not a spiritual virtue.

There are reasons why self-reliance, apparently honourable in the realm of furnishing our needs or those of a family, is not esteemed by God in the realm of relating to him.

One is that 'self-reliance' in practical and material matters is never the whole truth about even the most self-reliant of men and women. It is true we are to work to live, but our ability to work and the opportunity to work fruitfully are both God-given. Therefore, in the bigger picture, even the food on the table, which is the result of someone earning, someone buying and someone cooking, is the outworking of God's grace – that is God's giving. 'You may say to yourself, "My power and the strength of my hands have produced this wealth for me." But remember the Lord your God, for it is he who gives you the ability to produce wealth...'(Deut. 8:17-18). Even in this sphere of life we are wholly dependent on God's grace; God is the great provider, not man.

But secondly and importantly, in the making of material provision for ourselves and our families, we are commanded to do what we can do – which, in most cases, is work; the Bible nowhere commends laziness. Whereas in the spiritual realm we are commanded to come to terms with what we *cannot* do – we cannot keep God's law perfectly. This distinction between trying to do what we can do, whilst not presuming to do what we cannot do, is essential if we are to be those who hold out open hands to receive from God.

So here the first and essential ingredient of receiving a right standing with God as a gift from his hands: this right standing is not something we deserve or can achieve for ourselves.

2. This right standing with God comes '...through the redemption that came by Christ Jesus' (v. 24).

This right standing with God comes to us thanks to a rescue (or 'redemption') that God has accomplished at great cost to himself. For God to put us right with himself, he gave his Son to bear the judgment that our sins deserve in our place. The redemption came 'by Christ Jesus'.

This means that a person able to avail himself of what Jesus has done in dying on the cross will have no further guilt to bear in this life, and no further penalty to pay on judgment day or in the next.

There remains no further punishment for our sins; the penalty has been borne in full. And this applies equally to sins committed before Jesus died on the cross (here referred to as 'sins committed beforehand'), as to sins committed after Jesus died on the cross. It applies to sins I commit before I know of this death of Jesus in my place, and to sins I commit afterwards.

The death of Jesus has accomplished our rescue or redemption for three reasons given here:

*a. the death of Jesus was a **demonstration of God's justice** (vv. 25, 26).*

This was not because Jesus on the cross was being justly punished for his sins, for he was the sinless Son of God, and he had none. Rather, when he died on the cross he had *our* sins laid to *his* account, and *he* bore the punishment that *we* deserve in *our* place. In this way God rescues or redeems us without compromising his own perfectly just character.

*b. the death of Jesus was a **sacrifice of atonement** (v. 25).*

This means a sacrifice which turns aside God's anger. God's anger, unlike ours, is righteous anger – a right and measured reaction to our wrong. Now, at the cross,

God's anger – his own righteous reaction to wrong – was turned aside from man, and redirected against himself in the person of his Son. Wonderfully, God in the person of his Son, Jesus, bore the full weight of his own righteous anger against sinful man.

c.   the death of Jesus was for **the justification of sinners** *(vv. 24, 26).*

Indeed this was the whole reason why God gave his Son to die on a cross, and why Jesus was willing to do his Father's will and go to the cross. It was so that sinners like us might be freed from the just judgment of God which we do deserve, and instead be 'justified' – treated by God 'just-as-if-I'd' never sinned – which we do not deserve.

And notice that in speaking of us being 'justified', he is speaking of us here as those who 'have sinned and fall short of the glory of God' (Rom. 3:23). That is wonderful news! God is not in the business of justifying the really good people – 'saints' as we sometimes call them, but 'sinners', those who will acknowledge that they have sinned and fall far short of the glory of God. That's me – and it can be you too, whoever you are, wherever you are, whatever you've done.

So, in summary, the right standing with God, which we need, comes to us not by our observing and performing the requirements of God's law. Rather it comes to us as a rescue or redemption through Christ Jesus. We are rescued, or redeemed, as a result of God's just judgment on human sin falling on the sinless Son of God. As a result, God's anger is turned away from us, and he is able to 'justify' or acquit us, declaring us right in his sight – and all this without compromising his own pure and perfect justice.

3. *This right standing with God comes **through faith in Christ Jesus** (vv. 22, 26).*

It remains to ask whether this rescue, or redemption, for a right standing with God comes automatically to all people, regardless of whether we want it. Who is it that stands to gain life from the death of Jesus? Does God justify all people, whether or not they know of the redemption that came by Christ Jesus, and whether or not they care about him? Does God save a person who never acknowledges he needs saving?

The answer given here is that this right standing with God is received *'through faith'*, as the following two verses show (my emphasis added):

> 'This righteousness from God comes *through faith in Jesus Christ* to all who believe.' (v. 22)

> 'God presented him as a sacrifice of atonement...He did this to demonstrate his justice..., so as to be just and the one who justifies those who *have faith in Jesus.'* (v. 26)

Faith in Jesus is the key. But what is 'faith'? The word is used in a number of slightly different ways in the Bible. We can see what 'faith' means in a particular context by asking the question, 'what is faith being contrasted with?'

The answer here is that faith in *Jesus Christ,* and what *he* has done to put us right with God, is being contrasted with reliance on *ourselves* and what *we* may do to try to put ourselves back in the right with God. No attempt to put ourselves right with God by what we *do* can succeed. But, by contrast, abandoning self-reliance, and putting our trust (faith) in *Jesus* and what he has *done* in dying for us, is the way to be established in a right standing with God.

So to say we are 'justified' (declared in the right with God) *by faith in Jesus' death for us* is the positive counterpart to the negative we looked at earlier when we saw that our right standing with God comes to us *apart from law.* We are put into a right standing with God not on account of what we *do* for God, but on account of what God, in Christ, *has done* for us.

This is not complicated, but we human beings are complicated! As a result there are a number of common misunderstandings surrounding this key phrase *'through faith'.* Consider, for example, a number of possible responses to it:

'I admire your faith but I do not have this great faith, of which you speak.'

The answer to this is that 'faith' is really a matter of reliance or dependence. The only question is, what am I depending on for my right standing with God? By nature we all depend on – that is have faith in – ourselves, our own good lives or our own religious knowledge and performance. But God is saying 'do not depend on yourself; depend on me, and the redemption I have provided in my Son and his death on the cross'.

'Isn't faith a rather divisive and therefore undesirable thing?'

In one sense any claim to tell the truth divides people into those who accept the claim and those who reject it. And this apparent divisiveness of truth claims is not limited to those claims made by and for the Christian faith. Anyone who says all religions are false makes a 'truth claim', as does the person who says 'all religions are the same,' or indeed the person who says 'there is no such thing as an absolute truth.' All these are 'truth claims' and are divisive, however 'inclusive' they may be intended to sound.

However, importantly, the message of salvation from God, through Christ, is wonderfully uniting. It means that among God's people – all those who receive this salvation from God – there is absolute unity and equality.

Not only does the message of salvation put an end to personal pride, as we have seen, but it simultaneously makes all differences of race, class, wealth or education of no spiritual significance at all.

At the time of Jesus and the early church, there was a great divide between Jew and non-Jew (or Gentile). But the good news of salvation through Christ, for Jew and Gentile, broke down the barrier that existed between them.

And this message continues to break down barriers between people of different races, nations and backgrounds today. It truly includes and truly unites all those who look to Jesus and his death as the sole means of salvation from sin and judgment. There is no scope for any one-upman-ship or pride of place. The ground is level at the foot of the cross; the cross of Christ is the great leveller of mankind.

'Surely I must do something other than just believe?'
The short answer is that there is nothing I can do to save myself. Rather, God is honoured as I depend upon him to do for me, through Christ's death on the cross, all that he has promised. As has been said, 'All is of God; the only thing of my very own which I contribute to my redemption is the sin from which I need to be redeemed.[2]' The hymn writer, Isaac Watts, wrote:

> When I survey the wondrous cross
> On which the Prince of Glory died,
> My richest gain I count but loss,
> And pour contempt on all my pride.[3]

2　From 'Nature, Man and God' by William Temple, Archbishop of Canterbury, Gifford Lectures, 1934.

3　From Isaac Watts' hymn 'When I survey the wondrous cross', published in 1707 (the hymn of which Charles Wesley is reputed to have said he would give up all his other hymns to have written this one).

'Doesn't faith make a person rather proud?'

Perhaps Christians can appear rather proud or self-righteous. Some allowance needs to be made for the fact that not all who profess a faith are in fact depending on the death of Jesus for their acceptance with God. But the real question is, 'Does this way of salvation necessitate that those who trust in Christ become proud?' The answer, surely, is 'no'; to trust in Christ, and specifically in his death for my salvation, is the very opposite of being confident in – or proud of – myself.

Of course, those trusting in Christ will appear confident before God, and without any word of explanation that could look like self-confidence. But a person truly trusting in Christ ought to be quick to say, 'I am *not* confident in anything *I can do* to put myself right with God, but I am confident in what *Christ has done* for all who will trust in him'. 'Where, then, is boasting? It is excluded' (Rom. 3:27). Isaac Watts, again:

> Forbid it, Lord, that I should boast,
> Save in the death of Christ, my God;
> All the vain things that charm me most,
> I sacrifice them to his blood.

'I believe in Jesus, but I still can't be sure I am in the right with God.'

The answer to this is to ask, 'What do you believe in Jesus for?' It is possible to believe in Jesus for moral guidance, physical health or even spiritual illumination, and never really understand what the Bible plainly claims for Jesus, namely that *'God presented him as a sacrifice of atonement' (v. 25).*

But God is saying here that Christ Jesus is presented or set forth not merely as one who reveals truth to us as a spiritual guide (though he does), nor even as the one who reigns and therefore is powerful to protect from harm and give health (though he is). Of supreme importance here is that Christ is set forth as the one who redeems sinful men and women. And he does that by taking the just judgment that we deserve for our sin on himself. Knowing that Christ Jesus has borne the judgment in my place, and in full, is the way to be at peace with God now, and anticipate a welcome into his presence eternally.

'If God puts a person right with himself, only through a person depending on Christ and his cross, what incentive is there to live well?'

It is quite true, as we have seen, that the death of Christ pays for a person's sins, in a way that nothing else ever could. Having said that, receiving and rejoicing in God's mercy through Christ will have a life-changing effect on me. I shall experience a debt of gratitude to God, and I shall want to surrender my life to the service of the one who has had mercy on me.

This is indeed the proper and fitting response. But this *response* to God's grace must never be mistaken for the *reason* for God's grace. The reason for God's grace must never be sought and found in any good that I have done in the past or will do in the future, but only in the sheer goodness of God towards undeserving people like me. Again, Isaac Watts' hymn:

> Were the whole realm of Nature mine,
> That were an offering far too small;
> Love so amazing, so divine,
> Demands my soul, my life, my all.

******

No one passage of the Bible can adequately display the jewel that is the message of the cross. But consider five facets of this multifaceted jewel.

A first facet – a clean conscience.

All of us have a conscience. Consciences may be calibrated slightly differently, and some may be sensitive where others are untroubled. But at some point we all know the strain and stress of a guilty conscience. There are things we have done that we shouldn't have done, and there are things we haven't done that we should have done. What power on earth can clean up a dirty conscience? What can silence its accusations? The answer is only the message of the cross of Christ.

At the cross, God says, I know the worst about you, and I am able and willing to take the blame for your wrong, in the person of My Son. Look to Jesus and his cross.

In the years before Jesus came to live on earth and die on a cross, God had taught his people through a system of sacrifices that 'without the shedding of blood there is no forgiveness.' But those sacrifices merely pointed forward to the one perfect sacrifice of Christ for sins. Those sacrifices could not themselves secure the forgiveness of God for his people. And nor could they 'clear the conscience of the worshipper'. By contrast, the 'blood of Christ... will cleanse our consciences from acts that lead to death, so that we may serve the living God' (Heb. 9:9, 14, 22). 'Therefore, there is now no condemnation for those who are in Christ Jesus...'says the apostle Paul (Rom. 8:1).

The eighteenth-century hymn writer, Charles Wesley, famously expressed the joy of discovering Christ died for sins and for sinners:

And can it be that I should gain
An interest in the Saviour's blood?
Died he for me who caused his pain –
For me, who him to death pursued?
Amazing love! how can it be,
That thou, my God, shouldst die for me?

And in words more personal still, that hymn writer
recounts how this message struck him,

...my chains fell off, *my heart was free*,
I rose, went forth, and followed Thee.

A 'free heart' is a cleansed conscience. This is a first facet
of the jewel of the message of Christ's cross and it lifts
a very heavy burden from the troubled human heart.

A second facet – a living presence.
What wonderfully flows from a cleansed heart and
conscience is – amazingly – that God the Holy Spirit
is willing and able to take up residence in such a heart.
He, the Holy Spirit, is promised to all those who receive
the forgiveness of sins through the message of Christ's
cross,[4] and he makes real the presence of God, Father
and Son, in the life of the believer.[5]

The Holy Spirit is a 'person' (the Spirit *of God* or *of
Christ*) rather than a force, but one way in which his
living presence is experienced by a believer is in his
transforming power in a believer's life. As the Holy
Spirit makes real God's complete forgiveness to a person
trusting in the cross of Christ, the power of forgiven sin
is broken. Another of Charles Wesley's hymns expresses
this truth by saying *'He breaks the power of cancelled sin.'*

4   See Chapter 8.

5   Christians believe that the one God has revealed himself as Father, Son
and Holy Spirit. This is the Christian doctrine of the Trinity.

What exactly does this mean? Well, assuming the testimony of countless numbers of Christians is to be believed, it doesn't mean we don't experience the attractiveness of wrong or that we don't do wrong. But it does mean that sin, which gains its grip in my life through guilt, has its iron grip fatally weakened at the cross.

The voice of sin says, 'You're a guilty failure; you might as well give up.' The voice of the Spirit says, 'You're a forgiven sinner; you're free to grow up.' The voice of sin says, 'You're a "child of the devil"; follow him.' The voice of the Spirit says, 'You're a child of God; follow him'. Again, the voice of sin says 'You have no power to change.' The voice of the Spirit says, 'You have the presence and power of Almighty God at your disposal.'

And on what authority can the Holy Spirit say these things? The Holy Spirit speaks to the believer on the authority of God in Christ, who says Christ's death is sufficient to pay for all sin. His death cleanses the conscience, yes; and beyond that his death liberates the will.

Perhaps a Christian will feel he is making little progress in personal holiness and transformation of life. The apostle Peter identifies one clear reason why that may be so, namely that such a person 'is short-sighted and blind, and has forgotten that he has been cleansed from his past sins' (2 Pet. 1:9). The assurance of past sins forgiven is a key to present progress in godliness.

The living presence of God, Father and Son, by the Holy Spirit – this is a second facet of the jewel of the cross of Christ.

A third facet – a present access.

The problem with our sin and guilt is that it disqualifies us for a relationship with God. With just an ounce of awareness of God's moral perfection or holiness, and our moral and spiritual failure, we will know instinctively that we are not – and could never be – 'mates with God'.

By nature we simply do not have that essential purity of life and character to draw close to God.[6] Once we know that, we are better able to see just how wonderful is the message of the grace of God in the cross of Christ. For the cross of the Lord Jesus is, for the person trusting in him, the gateway into the presence of God:

> [1]Therefore, since we have been justified through faith, we have peace with God through our Lord Jesus Christ, [2]through whom we have gained access by faith into this grace in which we now stand. (Rom. 5:1-2)

The apostle Paul is here drawing out an application of the truth of 'justification by faith' which is *access to grace*'; that means *access* to God and all his goodness, and not least access to God in prayer. I can talk to the creator of the universe! And not just as a creature to his creator, or a subject to his sovereign, but as child to his or her father; Jesus taught his disciples to pray 'Our Father...'

So says another Bible writer:

> [19]Therefore, brothers, since we have confidence to enter the Most Holy Place [*the presence of God*] by the blood of Jesus, [20]by a new and living way opened for us through the curtain, that is, his body, [21]and since we have a great priest over the house of God, [22]let us draw near to God with a sincere heart in full assurance of faith, having our hearts sprinkled to cleanse us from a guilty conscience and having our bodies washed with pure water. (Heb. 10:19-22)

---

6   Psalm 15:1: 'LORD, who may dwell in your sanctuary? Who may live on your holy hill?' See also Isaiah 6:5.

The message of 'the blood of Jesus' is the key to a cleansed conscience and confident access into the presence of God. Prayer may not be easy for the Christian; we will be glad for all the help that is promised to us in the gift of God's Holy Spirit, but the death of Jesus gives us access into the presence of God in the here and now. A present access into the presence of God is a third facet of the jewel of the message of the cross of Christ.

A fourth facet – a secure future.
Access into the presence of God now anticipates access into the presence of God one day in the future. For the person trusting in Jesus, and his death, the future is secure.

> [9]Since we have now been justified by his blood, how much more shall we be saved from God's wrath through him! [10]For if, when we were God's enemies, we were reconciled to him through the death of his Son, how much more, having been reconciled, shall we be saved through his life! (Rom. 5:9-10)

Loosely paraphrased, the apostle Paul is saying 'since God has, through the death of his Son, accomplished the really difficult task of making his enemies into his friends, how much more will he take his friends home to heaven!' And this 'gospel logic' that commends itself to human reason will one day be evident to us in personal experience.

Be assured, the apostle is saying, heaven is not just a matter of wishful thinking. It is an assured consequence of the cross of Christ. When he died there, he took the penalty of the believer's sin in full, and therefore what awaits the believer is not a debt to be discharged but an inheritance to be enjoyed.

Therefore, the believer is to be free from fearful and anxious thoughts of a state of 'purgatory' or a sentence of condemnation, and live instead with the glad assurance that a wonderfully warm welcome into the presence of God awaits him. At the last, the Lord Jesus stands to save his people from his own righteous judgment, for he has borne that judgment in full at the cross.

A secure future is a fourth facet of this jewel of the message of the cross of Christ.

A fifth facet – a perfect qualification

A fifth facet of this jewel of the message of the cross is that the person trusting in the cross of Christ is credited with the perfect character of Jesus. It is not just that my sins are wiped away, but in their place Christ's perfection is made over to me.

This is indeed a 'sweet exchange', as many have called it. My sin is laid to Christ's account; and Christ's perfection, or righteousness, is credited to my account. The apostle Paul summarises this truth by saying, 'God made him who had no sin to be sin for us, so that in him we might become the righteousness of God' (2 Cor. 5:21).

Notwithstanding all we have seen in these last pages, perhaps the feeling overwhelms us that we will 'only just make it', and that having made it into heaven we shall skulk around in the background feeling peculiarly unqualified to be there at all. Rather like being the last person to be picked for a team, or the one who scrapes through the test by the skin of his teeth, or someone being rather underdressed at a smart party – many of us will know the feeling of being 'barely qualified' to be there.

So also when it comes to anticipating a future in God's presence, many could conjure up in our minds the sense of not really feeling qualified to be there. If we have grasped the truth about our own sinfulness and unworthiness before God, this feeling will be especially acute. We know there is no question of fronting up to God and asking him to add up our credits in the bank of heaven because of course we know this would not add up to much, especially with an awful lot of debits to take into account too.

But the truth we have been looking at points us in a completely different direction. It says *both* that the sins which *disqualify* us have been taken by Christ, and paid for by him, *and* that the perfect character of Christ which we need to *qualify* us to stand confidently and unashamed before God, is given to us. How wonderful is that!

Thanks to the goodness of God that comes to us through the cross of Christ, we need never feel like heaven's second-class citizens, only there to make up the numbers. Rather, we can know we are perfectly qualified to be there – not on account of a perfection we have achieved, but on account of the perfection which God in Christ has given to us. To return to the earlier analogies, it is like discovering we have scored full marks in the test, we have been the captain's first choice for membership of the team, we have the perfect set of clothes for the party – we have the perfect qualification to be there.

If God had a recording of my whole life, the prospect of judgment day would really be unbearable: every failure of thought, word and deed exposed before his eyes. But in fact when Jesus died on the cross, the recording of my every failure was seen by God and paid for then by him, in the person of his Son. As a result, when I face the judgment day, it will not be the recording of my imperfection that is the basis of God's judgment, but rather the recording of Christ's perfection that is the basis of God's judgment. As the apostle Paul writes, Jesus died for us so that '...in him [Jesus] we might become the righteousness of God'. The wonderful outcome will be my full and glad welcome into my heavenly Father's presence.

A perfect qualification is a fifth facet of this jewel of the message of the cross of Christ.

******

We are wary and suspicious of good news, and especially so when we seem to be being offered something for nothing. And 'justification by grace through faith' that we have been looking at in this chapter, is one such piece of – almost – unbelievably good news.

Indeed, it is hard to know which piece of news is harder to accept. Is it the bad news of human sinfulness which tells us that we are all much worse than we think we are? Or is it the good news of the grace of God who loved his unlovely world so much that he was willing to give his one and only son to die on a cross, to redeem, rescue and restore us to a relationship with him?

On balance, and strangely, it is probably the good news that is the harder of the two to believe. For human sinfulness is everywhere evident to us through all the conflicts and wars in our world, and all the broken and strained relationships of our lives. We have newspapers to tell us what is wrong out there and, more importantly, we have consciences that testify to our own wrong within. For all that I may have found ways of silencing my conscience – numbing it, placating it or accommodating it – it speaks still, and nags away. It tells me with unerring consistency that all is not well with my heart. All this makes the bad news of our human sinfulness a sad but believable truth.

The good news of the grace of God, however, is nothing that we could guess at. It is not a truth we can discover by listening to our hearts, or even by listening to our world. It is news that must come to us from God himself. We have heard how the Bible (God's Word, as Christians believe it to be) presents that good news from God. How do you respond to it?

Like all gifts that we are offered, we may respond by saying, 'I don't *need* it.' But if the bad news of our human condition is to be believed, can we honestly say that?

We may respond, 'I don't *want* it.' Perhaps we fear that receiving such a priceless gift from God will bring with it the indebtedness of gratitude, to live for him. And we may say we don't want *that*. But if God is so good as to love us by sending his Son to die for us, is this God not the only one for whom we would want to live?

Perhaps we respond by saying, 'I don't *believe* the message of God's grace.' The offer sounds too good to be true. A book like this can be a help or a hindrance in believing what the Bible is saying. It can be a help if it is some encouragement to meet with Christians and read the Bible. It can be a hindrance if it becomes a substitute for either or both. For my part, I needed to hear this message from the lips of a trustworthy Christian – which in God's goodness I did around the spring of 1977. And if this good news remains unbelievable for you, the next step might be to find a Bible-believer you can trust who can add their testimony to mine, and encourage you to 'taste and see that the Lord is good' (Ps. 34:8). Really good.

BIG QUESTIONS

JACK ASKS:
What about those who have never heard of Jesus?
It is fair to say that the Bible does not answer this
question explicitly, perhaps for a number of reasons.

First, because anyone looking in the Bible for an answer
to this question has, of course, heard of Jesus and the
question for all of us in that situation is, 'What will *we* do
with the Christ of whom *we* have heard?' rather than 'What
will God do with those who have not heard of salvation
through his Son?' And we should think to ourselves, how
good God is – not only to love me as he has, in sending his
Son to live and then to die for me – but also how good God
is to bring the message of the cross of Christ to me! Some
will *hope* that God will be merciful to them; but knowing
Jesus died on the cross for undeserving sinners, I can be
sure that in belonging to this Jesus, God will be merciful
to me. This is amazing grace! How, then, will I respond to
what I now know of God's goodness to me?

Second, once we have heard the good news that
Christians believe, we become part of the answer to
the question, 'How shall others hear?' Therefore, a real
concern, as opposed to a merely academic interest in the
fate of those who have not heard about Jesus, will show
itself in doing all we can to enable them to hear of Jesus
and receive salvation from him. Many of us will have
family and friends, neighbours and colleagues, and all
these people have a better opportunity to trust in Christ
as a result of our being able to tell them. One writer
put it this way: '...in the meantime, if you are worried
about the people outside, the most unreasonable thing
you can do is to remain outside yourself. Christians are

Christ's body, the organism through which he works. Every addition to that body enables him to do more. If you want to help those outside you must add your own little cell to the body of Christ who can help them. Cutting off a man's fingers would be an odd way of getting him to do more work.'[7]

Finally, the shortest and best answer to this question concerning how God will deal with other people is that he will do right. If God can be trusted to save us, are we not right to trust God to act justly with his world? As one man of God exclaimed, 'Will not the Judge of all the earth do right?'(Gen. 18:25)

---

7   C.S. Lewis, *Mere Christianity*, p. 53.

7 How can I know God?

The end of all learning is to know God, and out of that knowledge to love and imitate him.

JOHN MILTON

I tell you the truth, no-one can see the kingdom of God unless he is born again.

JESUS OF NAZARETH

We were made for a relationship with God. But that relationship has been broken; from our side, because we have rebelled against God and, in consequence, from his side, because we are under his judgment. How shall the relationship with God, for which we were made, be restored? Augustine famously said 'You have made us for yourself, O Lord, and our hearts are restless until they rest in you.[1]' How, then, shall our hearts be at rest in him and at peace with him?

Jesus said we need to be born again. At any rate, that was how Jesus explained our need to one religious man who did not yet know God and had not yet experienced spiritual reality as God intends for us:

> [1]Now there was a man of the Pharisees named Nicodemus, a member of the Jewish ruling council. [2]He came to Jesus at night and said, 'Rabbi, we know you are a teacher who has come from God. For no-one could perform the miraculous signs you are doing if God were not with him.'

---

1   From *Confessions* by St Augustine of Hippo, written A.D. 397-8.

³In reply Jesus declared, 'I tell you the truth, no-one can see the kingdom of God unless he is born again.'

⁴'How can a man be born when he is old?' Nicodemus asked. 'Surely he cannot enter a second time into his mother's womb to be born!'

⁵Jesus answered, 'I tell you the truth, no-one can enter the kingdom of God unless he is born of water and the Spirit. ⁶Flesh gives birth to flesh, but the Spirit gives birth to spirit. ⁷You should not be surprised at my saying, "You must be born again." ⁸The wind blows wherever it pleases. You hear its sound, but you cannot tell where it comes from or where it is going. So it is with everyone born of the Spirit'. (John 3:1-8)

A SPIRITUAL BIRTH

Nicodemus has clearly witnessed some of the miracles Jesus performed and he concludes that Jesus is a teacher who has come from God. But Jesus breaks in to say to Nicodemus that unless and until he is born again, he will neither see nor enter the kingdom of God. In other words, Nicodemus, who comes to Jesus one dark evening, is in spiritual darkness too. And more than that, this 'new birth' that Jesus says the well educated Jewish Nicodemus needs, is also indispensable for every man, woman and child born into this world. Of course it is not a second physical birth that we need; it is a *spiritual birth* as Jesus repeatedly makes plain:

'...I tell you the truth, no-one can see the kingdom of God unless he is born again.' (v. 3)

'I tell you the truth, no-one can enter the kingdom of God unless he is born of water and the Spirit.' (v. 5)

'Flesh gives birth to flesh, but the Spirit gives birth to spirit.' (v. 6)

'...So it is with everyone born of the Spirit.' (v. 8)

How are we to understand the working of the Spirit? It is analogous, Jesus says, to the blowing of the wind – in two respects. First, Jesus is saying the Spirit (of God), like the wind, is not under the control of man. The Spirit blows where he pleases, just as the wind blows wherever it pleases (v. 8). Therefore, no-one can make the Spirit work to bring a person to Christ:

> 'The wind blows wherever it pleases. You hear its sound, but you cannot tell where it comes from or where it is going. So it is with everyone born of the Spirit.' (v. 8)

Secondly, however, just as when the wind blows you witness its effects ('*You hear its sound...*' and, for example, see the waving of tree branches or the filling of the sails of a boat), so also in the same way we can detect where the Spirit of God has been at work. In the verses that follow we are given two signs of the Spirit of God at work in the lives of people. The first sign of the Spirit at work in my life is:

I AM TRUSTING IN JESUS' DEATH

> [14]Just as Moses lifted up the snake in the desert, so the Son of Man must be lifted up, [15]that everyone who believes in him may have eternal life. [16]For God so loved the world that he gave his one and only Son, that whoever believes in him shall not perish but have eternal life. [17]For God did not send his Son into the world to condemn the world, but to save the world through him. (John 3:14-17)

The first sign Jesus gives of a sovereign work of the Spirit of God in the life of an individual is that the person is found to be trusting in the death of Jesus. This was the theme of the last chapter; it was also, says Jesus, the essential truth being taught by God, through Moses, in an incident in the Old Testament. The Israelites in the desert are being fatally bitten by snakes. God instructs Moses to lift up a bronze snake on a pole, and then tell the people to look at the snake on the pole. When they look at the snake on the pole, they will be healed and live.[2] In the same way, Jesus says that the Son of Man (his own favourite name for himself) must be 'lifted up' (that is, on a cross, to die), 'so that everyone who believes in him may have eternal life' (v. 15).

The link between these two events is that in each case there is a 'lifting' and a 'looking'. The snake is *lifted* up on the pole; the Son of Man is *lifted* up on a cross. So too, the Israelite was to *look*, and see, on the pole, the snake that had bitten him; and today we are to *look*, and see, on the cross, the sin that has crippled us. How so? By recognizing that on the cross, 'God made him who had no sin to be sin for us... ,'(2 Cor. 5:21) as on the cross Jesus carried our sin, and bore the judgment we deserve in our place.

The cross is the famous symbol of the Christian faith. But not all who see a cross look with understanding and see that the one lifted up to die carried our sin, and bore its judgment, as he died. However, when we look with understanding at the cross, and believe in Jesus as the one who bore the sins of the world, and more specifically still as the one who bore *my sins*, then the cross becomes the power to save us from death and bring us to eternal life.

Illuminated by Scripture, the cross of Christ tells us the *extent* of God's love for us. 'For God so loved the world that he gave his one and only Son...' (v. 16)

---

2   'The LORD said to Moses, "Make a snake and put it up on a pole; anyone who is bitten can look at it and live." So Moses made a bronze snake and put it up on a pole. Then when anyone was bitten by a snake and looked at the bronze snake, he lived' (Num. 21:8-9).

and again, 'God did not send his Son into the world to condemn the world, but to save the world through him' (v. 17). This truth is unchanging.

But the cross of Christ is not only a proclamation of unchanging truth; it is also an invitation to life-changing trust or faith for 'whoever believes in him shall not perish but have eternal life' (v. 16). It is not that 'faith' is a personal religious achievement that saves us. On the contrary, looking *to* Christ on the cross as the one who can be trusted to save us involves looking *away* from ourselves, and turning aside from any ability we think we may have to save ourselves.

Trusting in Jesus' death is the first sign that the Spirit of God has been at work in our lives in a saving way. There is a second sign of the Spirit at work in my life:

I AM TURNING TO FOLLOW THE LIFE OF JESUS

The second sign of the Spirit of God at work to save me is that I am turned to following Christ with my life. In other words, there is a moral dimension to belonging to Jesus; it has to do not only with trusting him as the one who claimed to die for us – as we have just seen – but also obeying him as the one who claims to be the light to guide and direct our lives:

> [18]Whoever believes in him is not condemned, but whoever does not believe stands condemned already because he has not believed in the name of God's one and only Son. [19]This is the verdict: Light has come into the world, but men loved darkness instead of light because their deeds were evil. (John 3:18-19)

The good news is that the Spirit of God can do for us what we are not able or inclined to do for ourselves; he can cause us to want to live by the truth, rather than lies, and to live by the light, rather than live in the darkness.

The sign that the Spirit of God is at work in us is that he causes us to acknowledge Jesus as the light of the world, and to come to him for his light to direct our lives:

> [20]Everyone who does evil hates the light, and will not come into the light for fear that his deeds will be exposed. [21]But whoever lives by the truth comes into the light, so that it may be seen plainly that what he has done has been done through God. (John 3:20-21)

This may seem rather unremarkable. After all, everyone has a moral code for life, and surely our code for life pretty well matches God's required standard. Is not my life a fair reflection of God's light? And also, light can sound like the thing we seek, rather than that from which instinctively we hide; if asked, we all prefer to live in the light rather than in darkness.

But in fact whereas many of us seek light in the sense of guidance for life's decisions, Jesus is saying it is not natural to us – even in circumstances where we seek such guidance – to seek to be governed by the perfect purity of Christ's character and commands. We are, by nature, like the beetles under the stone in the garden; we are allergic to the light. When the stone is lifted and daylight exposes us, we run from the light, hide from it and shun it.

However, when the Spirit of God does his work of bringing me to new birth, that instinct changes. When that happens, I have a new desire to live by the light; I am ready then for the truth to chase away the lies, and the light to drive away the darkness under which evil thoughts, words and deeds have taken cover.

...AND WITHOUT THE SPIRIT OF GOD?

We have looked at two signs of the Holy Spirit at work, but without the Spirit of God at work in a person, life will be very different. I cannot do either of these two things; I will neither be trusting in the death of Jesus nor will I be turned to follow the light of Jesus.

Very likely we will rationalise our position by saying we need to know that the Bible is true before we follow Jesus. In fact, however, the reverse is the case: we need to be willing to follow Jesus before we will know the Bible is true. Jesus said, 'If anyone chooses to do God's will, he will find out whether my teaching comes from God or whether I speak on my own' (John 7:17). So I am caught: I don't want to obey without believing; Jesus says I won't be able to believe without obeying. Why would God put us in such an impossible situation?

The answer is that without the Spirit of God we are not the impartial, detached observers and unbiased analysts that we imagine ourselves to be. On the contrary, Jesus tells us here that we have a bias towards evil, and a vested interest in extinguishing the light that would expose our evil deeds. For all of us it is more comfortable and convenient to stay away from the light that would show us up for what we really are. And one good way of shielding ourselves from Jesus, the light, is not to come to him or, as we would say 'not to believe in him'. But in doing so we show we are guilty:

> This is the verdict: light has come into the world, but men loved darkness instead of light because their deeds were evil. (John 3:19)

...BUT WITH THE SPIRIT OF GOD?

So, I greatly need the Holy Spirit to be at work in me. The new birth of every individual is a sovereign and invisible work of the Spirit of God in the human heart. We have seen here that there are two tangible consequences in the life of an individual. The first is that I *trust* in the death of Christ; this becomes the sole ground of my confidence before God. And the second is that I *turn* to follow the light of Christ; his life and teaching, made real to me by the Spirit of God, increasingly shape the desires of my heart and the direction of my life.

These two signs of the Spirit's work, *trusting* and *turning*, can be identified and discussed separately, but they always and forever belong together. It is not so much that I cannot 'turn' my way of living without an effective 'trusting' in the death of Christ – though that is true. Nor even is it the case that I will never really be found 'trusting' in the death of Christ without also being committed to living Christ's way – though that will be true too. It is more simply that the Spirit of God will not make the mistake of leaving his sovereign work in the human heart half done. Where he brings a person to new birth, that person will be found both to be *trusting in* the death of Christ and *turning to* the light of Christ.

We might ask whether the person who 'trusts' and 'turns' is really qualitatively different from any individual who, to a degree, is God-fearing and clean-living. Commonly a person might say (or feel) 'I am a Christian (or a believer), but not a very good one.' The suspicion lurks that Christians divide into the 'nominal' and the 'committed', and that even the 'committed' sub-divide into the earnest and the really enlightened (or 'born-again'). And perhaps some will try to divide the born-again into the 'conservative' and the 'charismatic'.

None of these terms need defining, because none of the distinctions are here made by Jesus. These distinctions are not only not legitimate, they are positively damaging. They feed pride in those who feel they are a cut above the rest, and they discourage and disqualify others whom Christ has made his own. Either way, they take away from the work of Christ, by which alone we are saved. They also take away from the significance of the only distinction which Christ here makes. That distinction is between those who are born again by the Spirit of God, and those who are not. Put another way, it is a distinction which divides us into those who do know God and those who do not.

This distinction not only divides now, but it will endure eternally, and this is clear in the contrasting consequences that Jesus identifies for the believer and the unbeliever respectively:

> For God so loved the world that he gave his one and only Son, that whoever believes in him shall not perish but have eternal life. (John 3:16)

Eternal life is a relationship with God and his Son, Jesus Christ – not just more time to kill, but more life to live. So, elsewhere Jesus will say, 'now this is eternal life: that they may know you, the only true God, and Jesus Christ, whom you have sent' (John 17:3). Therefore, 'eternal life' is not in the first instance a quantity of time, but a quality of life.

But certainly the point is that this relationship enjoyed in this life continues eternally, whereas the person who does not know God, and who remains condemned, perishes.

These contrasting consequences point to believers and unbelievers as occupying utterly different positions – black and white – rather than existing in so many different shades of grey. Notice then that the *effect* of Christ's coming into the world is to divide us into those who follow him and those who reject him. And yet we mustn't get the impression that Jesus is indifferent to which side of that line we fall – with him or without him. Still less that it is his *intention* to condemn us. He tells us and he shows us that he came to save us!

> For God did not send his Son into the world to condemn the world, but to save the world through him. (John 3:17)

These twin responses of 'trusting' and 'turning' are the responses from our side which indicate a true work of the Spirit of God in our hearts. And for us, no less than for Nicodemus, this true work of the Spirit is the only way to know God. What Jesus said to Nicodemus, he says to us:

> I tell you the truth, no-one can see the kingdom of God unless he is born again. (John 3:3)

BIG QUESTIONS

JILL ASKS:
What am I supposed to feel at the end of this chapter?

JONATHAN ANSWERS:
Three things: First, Jesus' teaching will have left Nicodemus knowing he is *lifeless* spiritually. We should feel the same. Despite all his learning and insight – even insight into the person of Jesus – he is being told he needs a 'new birth' before he can see or enter the kingdom of God. It is the same for each of us.

Second, Nicodemus was being shown he was spiritually *powerless*. There is nothing a person can do to bring him or herself to spiritual life. This needful new birth is 'from above' or 'by the Spirit of God'. We, likewise, should be humbled by our powerlessness, spiritually speaking.

But, third, this teaching should leave us feeling spiritually *hopeful,* because God is in the business of bringing the spiritually dead to spiritual birth, and doing so by a power which is his and not theirs. If we recognise ourselves as being spiritually lifeless and powerless, the good news that comes to us from our creator God is that he can bring us to new birth.

JACKS ASKS:
What must I do? Just wait for God to do for me something I cannot do for myself?

JONATHAN ANSWERS:
Not exactly. Alongside Jesus teaching Nicodemus that he needs a new spiritual birth, Jesus is teaching the importance for us of:

Listening:
To the extent that Nicodemus did not understand these things, the remedy was to be found in listening to the one who knows:

> I tell you the truth, we speak of what we know, and we testify to what we have seen... (John 3:11)

In other words, Jesus speaks of things that he alone knows and understands, and we need, therefore, to *listen* to him.

Looking:

> [14]Just as Moses lifted up the snake in the desert, so the Son of Man must be lifted up, [15]that everyone who believes in him may have eternal life. (John 3:14-15)

The point is the Son of Man is to be 'lifted up' (to die on a cross), and Jesus is telling me to look at him. Why is Jesus giving up his life? So that my life and yours need not be forfeit! He is taking the judgment we deserve, in our place. So, *look* at the cross of Christ! And *learn* from the cross of Christ!

Loving and Leaving:

> [19]This is the verdict: Light has come into the world, but men loved darkness instead of light because their deeds were evil. [20]Everyone who does evil hates the light, and will not come into the light for fear that his deeds will be exposed. (John 3:19-20)

I am to make a sober estimate of the cost of belonging to Jesus. It is going to involve leaving things behind that I love. These will be things that I love, but that Christ does not. In some cases these things will be good gifts of God that I am abusing.

Drink, for example, is God's gift; drunkenness is its abuse. Sex is a good gift of our creator God to cement a marriage; outside a commitment in marriage it is misused. Money is a good gift to be used generously and wisely; greed is its misuse. Food is a good gift to enjoy; gluttony is its misuse. Humour is a good gift; sarcasm, coarse joking and mockery can be cruel and loveless. Power is often a God-given responsibility; tyranny is its corrupt use. Self-care is our duty – to care for the minds and bodies God has given us; obsessive self-grooming is vain. Work is the harnessing of our capacities and capabilities to care for God's world; workaholism is an idol.

By nature I love what Christ calls me to leave. Now is the time to weigh up the cost of leaving the things which I love, but which Christ does not.

How can I know God?

****

This chapter has been mainly about one conversation that took place between Jesus and one man, Nicodemus. The final chapter of this book will again look at a conversation between Jesus and one man, albeit a very different man to the religiously inclined Nicodemus.

Between these two chapters, we will look at one of the early Christian 'sermons', 'addresses', 'talks' or 'speeches' – call them what you will.

Few of us will be able to recall many – if any – life-changing talks that we have heard. Talks given in public are hard to hear. Often they seem too long. Often they don't seem too relevant. Often they are hard to understand. Often they leave us unmoved.

But the address we look at now, given in front of a large crowd, mainly of Jewish people, shortly after Jesus died and rose from the dead, was life-changing for approximately three thousand people. Why so?

First, because the things said were *convincing* to the minds of those listening, as explanation was given concerning the life, death and resurrection of Jesus.

Second, because the hearers were not just convinced in their minds, they were also *'cut to the heart';* they realised they were morally culpable as well as intellectually mistaken.

Third, because the things said *compelled* a response; the people listening said to the one speaking, and those standing with him, *'What shall we do?'*

If you had the opportunity to listen in to that kind of talk, would you listen? It is a talk that was first given on the day of Pentecost – a day that brought many Jews to Jerusalem for the celebration of a major Jewish festival

– and is recorded for us in the Acts of the Apostles. It was also the day on which the risen Lord Jesus fulfilled his promise[3] to send the Holy Spirit to his disciples. We're going to listen to that talk again. It was a life-changing message then and, when heard rightly, it is a life-changing message today.

---

3   See, for example, Luke 24:49: "'I am going to send you what my Father has promised; but stay in the city until you have been clothed with power from on high.'" See also John 7:37-39; 14:15-16.

A life-changing message

With many other words he warned them; and he pleaded with them, 'Save yourselves from this corrupt generation.' Those who accepted his message were baptised, and about three thousand were added to their number that day.

ACTS 2:40-41

Neither you nor I were there on the day of Pentecost when the Holy Spirit came on the disciples. We were not there to witness the accompanying miracles performed on that day.

But we do have an eyewitness account recorded by an early disciple, Luke.[1] And we do have an explanation of the events of that day given by the apostle Peter.

Luke records the events:

[1]When the day of Pentecost came, they were all together in one place. [2]Suddenly a sound like the blowing of a violent wind came from heaven and filled the whole house where they were sitting. [3]They saw what seemed to be tongues of fire that separated and came to rest on each of them. [4]All of them were filled with the Holy Spirit and began to speak in other tongues as the Spirit enabled them.

---

1   Luke was not one of the twelve apostles, but he was the missionary companion of Paul, and is the author of Luke's Gospel and the Acts of the Apostles.

> [5]Now there were staying in Jerusalem God-fearing Jews from every nation under heaven. [6]When they heard this sound, a crowd came together in bewilderment, because each one heard them speaking in his own language. [7]Utterly amazed, they asked: 'Are not all these men who are speaking Galileans? [8]Then how is it that each of us hears them in his own native language... [11b]we hear them declaring the wonders of God in our own tongues!' [12]Amazed and perplexed, they asked one another, 'What does this mean?'
>
> [13]Some, however, made fun of them and said, 'They have had too much wine'. (Acts 2:1-13)

The apostle Peter (one of Jesus' twelve disciples) gives the answer to the question: 'What do these miracles mean?' One suggestion made at that time is that they mean nothing – only that the disciples have had too much to drink. But Peter stands up to address the crowds and starts by saying the disciples are not drunk – it's only nine in the morning! No, rather, the disciples have received the Holy Spirit from God in fulfilment of what Joel, one Old Testament prophet, had predicted: 'In the last days, God says, I will pour out my Spirit on all people' (Acts 2:17).

Here is how Peter continues his speech:

> [22]'Men of Israel, listen to this: Jesus of Nazareth was a man accredited by God to you by miracles, wonders and signs, which God did among you through him, as you yourselves know. [23]This man was handed over to you by God's set purpose and foreknowledge; and you, with the help of wicked men, put him to death by nailing him to the cross. [24]But God raised him from the dead, ... because it was impossible for death to keep its hold on him. [25]David said about him:
>
> "I saw the Lord always before me.
> Because he is at my right hand, I will not be shaken.

[26]Therefore my heart is glad and my tongue rejoices;
my body also will live in hope,
[27]because you will not abandon me to the grave,
nor will you let your Holy One see decay.
[28]You have made known to me the paths of life;
you will fill me with joy in your presence."

[29]"Brothers, I can tell you confidently that the patriarch David died and was buried, and his tomb is here to this day. [30]But he was a prophet and knew that God had promised him on oath that he would place one of his descendants on his throne. [31]Seeing what was ahead, he spoke of the resurrection of the Christ, that he was not abandoned to the grave, nor did his body see decay. [32]God has raised this Jesus to life, and we are all witnesses of the fact. [33]Exalted to the right hand of God, he has received from the Father the promised Holy Spirit and has poured out what you now see and hear. [34]For David did not ascend to heaven, and yet he said,

"The LORD said to my Lord: 'Sit at my right hand
[35]until I make your enemies a footstool for your feet.'"

[36]"Therefore let all Israel be assured of this: God has made this Jesus, whom you crucified, both Lord and Christ.' (Acts 2:22-36)

Don't be discouraged by what, at first sight, seems hard to understand here. Peter may not here be addressing the questions on our minds, but he is addressing the question on the minds of those to whom he is speaking, namely, 'why are these miracles happening?' And the implications for us will soon be plain enough. Peter has in his speech a message for the mind, a message for the heart and a message to change a life.

(a) a message for the mind
Peter has said the explanation for the miracles that the people have witnessed is that the Holy Spirit has come

on all God's people. Now he explains why the Holy Spirit has come on God's people at this particular time. And the answer, says Peter, lies in the coming of the 'Christ' – the King that God had promised his people. It is *he* who has now sent his Spirit to his disciples.

Peter therefore recites the events concerning the life, death, resurrection, ascension and exaltation of Jesus, culminating in the pouring out of the Holy Spirit on the disciples – to establish the truth of the claim that 'God has made this Jesus, whom you crucified, both Lord and Christ' (v. 36).

Peter explains that at each point of Jesus' journey from heaven to earth and back to heaven again, God has borne witness to Jesus' uniqueness, in a way that marks him out as the promised 'Christ': See how the apostle Peter now shows the significance of:

- Jesus' life
- Jesus' death
- Jesus' resurrection
- Jesus' exaltation
- Jesus' giving of the Holy Spirit

First, Jesus' *life* points to Jesus as the Christ:

> 'Men of Israel, listen to this: Jesus of Nazareth was a man accredited by God to you by miracles, wonders and signs, which God did among you through him, as you yourselves know.' (Acts 2:22)

He is saying Jesus' miracles put us on notice that Jesus was marked out by God as special. That is why Mark (as we saw in ch. 3) recounts Jesus' astonishing feats of power. It is why John, in his Gospel, recounts Jesus' miracles and concludes: '...these are written that you may believe that Jesus is the Christ, the Son of God...' (see ch. 4).

Second, Jesus' *death* points to Jesus as the Christ:

> This man [Jesus] was handed over to you by God's set
> purpose and foreknowledge. (v. 23)

This is a real surprise. At first glance, the death of
Jesus looks so ordinary; execution by crucifixion was
common. But Peter says this crucifixion was not simply
an execution by men, but a 'handing over' by God. In
other words, the death of Jesus on a cross that appeared
to be simply the bad work of wicked men was in fact
also the good plan of a gracious God. And as we know
from subsequent speeches in the book of Acts, God's
good plan was to bring salvation, through the *death* of
his Son (as we saw in ch. 6).

Thirdly, Jesus' *resurrection* points to Jesus as the
Christ:

> But God raised him from the dead, freeing him from
> the agony of death, because it was impossible for death
> to keep its hold on him. (v. 24)

We looked at the resurrection of Jesus in chapter 4, but
one further reason in Peter's mind why it was impossible
for death to 'keep its hold on Jesus' will have been that
Scripture predicted the resurrection of the Christ. And
that was a prophecy which, until the coming of Jesus,
remained unfulfilled. King David, for example, the most
famous of Israel's kings could lay no claim to being
resurrected from the dead and preserved from the decay
of the grave; on the contrary, King David's grave (with
David's corpse) was plain for all to see.

But Jesus' tomb was empty and that was one more
vital clue that this Jesus was indeed the promised,
resurrected Christ. God raised Jesus, and in this way
King David's prophecy regarding the Christ who was to
come was fulfilled.

Fourth, Jesus' *exaltation* points to Jesus as the Christ:

> [34]For David did not ascend to heaven, and yet he said, 'The LORD said to my Lord: "Sit at my right hand [35]until I make your enemies a footstool for your feet".'(vv. 34-35, quoting Ps. 110:1)

Once again, Peter is putting his (predominantly Jewish) audience in mind of a Jewish prophecy. This prophecy was to the effect that God would cause someone to be exalted to, and seated at, his right hand – that is, the place of equal standing and authority to him.

But that prophecy of King David's was not fulfilled in himself for, as Peter remarks, 'David did *not* ascend to heaven.' No, once again, he spoke of what God would do for a greater king than David, a descendant who was yet to come. To that greater king, God would say, 'Sit at my right hand until I make your enemies a footstool for your feet.'

Now, says Peter, that prophecy has been fulfilled in the resurrection and exaltation of Jesus to God's right hand. Here, too, Jesus is marked out as the Christ.

Finally, Jesus receiving and *pouring out the Spirit* marks out Jesus as the Christ:

> Exalted to the right hand of God, he has received from the Father the promised Holy Spirit and has poured out what you now see and hear. (v. 33)

What the people now saw and heard, which required an explanation, was the coming of the Holy Spirit on the disciples, causing them to speak in other tongues and enabling the crowds to hear the disciples glorifying God in their own native tongues.

We saw earlier (ch. 3) that the gift of the Spirit was to be a hallmark distinguishing the ministry of the Christ from that of his illustrious forerunner, John the Baptist.

John himself had explained: 'I baptise you with water, but he will baptise you with the Holy Spirit' (Mark 1:8).

Therefore, says Peter, the best explanation for the events of Pentecost is that Jesus has received the Holy Spirit from the Father, and has poured out that same Spirit on the disciples. And this, too, marks Jesus out as the promised Christ.

So then, at every point, whether in the life of Jesus, or his death, his resurrection or ascension, his exaltation or the receiving and resulting pouring out of the Holy Spirit, God has been bearing witness to his Son as the promised *Christ*. So Peter concludes, drawing our attention to what we must not miss:

> Therefore let all Israel be assured of this: God has made this Jesus, whom you crucified, both Lord and Christ. (v. 36)

That is Peter's message for the mind; all the evidence points this way: Jesus is the promised Lord and Christ.

(b) a message for the heart

For us living 2,000 and more years after these historical events, none of this seems so relevant or moving. Not so relevant, because most of us are not living on the lookout for 'the Christ' (as in fact faithful Jews were); not so moving, because we were not there to witness the historical events of the rejection and execution of Jesus.

But on that day of Pentecost when the Spirit of God came on Jesus' disciples, which was the final and crowning piece of evidence that Jesus was indeed the expected Christ, Peter's explanation of events begins to pierce the hearts of his hearers. For the plain truth is that the overwhelming majority of those who had had the privilege of knowing Jesus, and the opportunity to believe in him as the promised Saviour-King of God's

189

people, reached exactly the wrong conclusion about him. This wrong assessment is seen in all its starkness in the contrast of that verse just quoted: 'God has made this Jesus, whom you crucified, both Lord and Christ'(Acts 2:36).

The people had executed him as a criminal. But God had resurrected and exalted him to his own right hand – in short, vindicated him as the Christ. Here was a message for the mind that was beginning to penetrate the hearts of Peter's listeners: the man you crucified was the Christ.

Humanly speaking, there had been a terrible miscarriage of justice. But more serious still is the spiritual blindness that enabled the Jewish nation[2] to miss the fact that God had indeed sent to them their 'Christ' (in Hebrew the word is 'Messiah'). It was a culpable blindness, and Peter's audience begin to recognise their guilt:

> When the people heard this, they were cut to the heart and said to Peter and the other apostles, 'Brothers, what shall we do?' (Acts 2:37)

When they ask 'What shall we do', they cannot be asking 'what can we do to undo the damage we have done?' There is no way guilty men can make amends for murderous actions by resurrecting their victims. For a start, death cannot be undone by mere men. Besides which, Peter has announced and explained that God has already resurrected the crucified Jesus; 'God has raised this Jesus to life, and we are all witnesses of the fact' (Acts 2:32).

---

2   Obviously not all Jewish people were involved directly in the decision to crucify Jesus, but those gathered in Jerusalem for Pentecost ('God-fearing Jews from every nation under heaven') are addressed corporately and take responsibility corporately: 'Fellow Jews and all of you who live in Jerusalem', 'Men of Israel', 'Brothers', concluding, 'Therefore let all Israel be assured of this: God has made this Jesus, whom you crucified, both Lord and Christ' (Acts 2:36).

No, the question 'What shall we do?' is not a question about undoing the past, but escaping the punishment and finding forgiveness for it.

If ever there were doubt about the availability of salvation for sinners, it is surely found here. Can even those very people who, humanly speaking, crucified the Christ be saved?

Many a sensitive conscience, half remembering and trying unsuccessfully to forget some incidents in the past, will battle with what is essentially the same question. *Can I be saved?* I have been blind; can I now be saved? I have been bad; can I now be saved? I have reached wrong conclusions, and spent a lifetime living out mistaken beliefs; can I now be saved? In my mind I have long since rejected Jesus as the Saviour of this world; can he now save me?

Others of us are not so consciously 'cut to the heart'. We acknowledge we are not perfect, of course, but we perhaps comfort ourselves that we are not criminals. We are not as good as some, but we feel better than others. At root, however, we have the same problem which is that we have lived without reference to the God who made us, who claims us as his own, and who has now sent his Son to this world to be our Lord. We have lived without reference to this God; can he now save us?

This is the question in their hearts: 'what shall we do?' Can we be saved? This is the 'heart' question Peter's message addresses.

(c) a message to change a life
The answer Peter gives to the stricken hearts of his hearers, 'Can I be saved?' is a resounding 'yes'. And now we find the apostle Peter outlining two observable steps by which his hearers can be reconciled to the God they have spurned. Here, in two words, is his message to change a life.

REPENT

This word conjures up a multitude of different meanings for different people which are not all helpful. Note that repentance is not primarily to do with the way I feel, nor is it in the first instance to do with the way I behave. The command to 'repent' is to *change our minds*; to admit that we have been wrong, and to change our thinking about Jesus.

Here on the day of Pentecost, this is what Peter commands the crowds to do. It is evident to Peter as he speaks, and to the crowds as they listen to him, that up until now they have reached entirely the wrong conclusion about Jesus. For them, Jesus was a blasphemer; he – a man – presumed to take the place and exercise the prerogatives of almighty God[3] and of the Christ.[4] But listening to Peter they can now see that God *has* made this Jesus 'both Lord and Christ'. God has indeed come to this earth in the person of Jesus: Jesus is the Lord. And Jesus is indeed God's anointed ruler of this world: Jesus is the Christ. The issue is not that Jesus is a blasphemer but that they have not been believers in him as Lord and Christ.

Therefore the crowd's first response must be to 'repent', which means to change their thinking about Jesus. It will also be the first and right response *we* make to the good news concerning Jesus; we need to 'repent', and change our thinking about him. Of course, this will have implications for the way we live. If Jesus is indeed the Lord and Christ, the rightful ruler of this world, then he must surely be the rightful ruler of my life. And

---

3   e.g. Mark 2:7 'He's blaspheming! Who can forgive sins but God alone?' Mark 14:63 'Why do we need any more witnesses? You have heard the blasphemy.' See chapter 3.

4   'They said, "He saved others; let him save himself if he is the Christ of God, the Chosen One"' (Luke 23:35).

my life will have a new direction, because it has in the Lord Jesus a new 'director'.

It will be a mistake, however, to imagine that the call to repent can be met by submitting to a code consisting of a few dos and don'ts; it's a whole new *direction* that is called for. To repent is to honour Jesus for who he is – the ruler of this world and the rightful ruler of my life. And that is a change of perspective that will bring a whole new way of thinking and living in its wake, over the course of a lifetime.

'Repent', then, is the first word describing a right response to the truth that Jesus is the ruler of this world. The second word that describes the appropriate response to the life-changing truth about Jesus is 'receive'.

RECEIVE

How is the rule of Jesus as Lord to be established in my life? Surprisingly, the rule of the Lord Jesus is experienced as I receive two gifts from him. The first is the forgiveness of my sins. The second is the gift of the Holy Spirit to dwell within me:

> 'Repent and be baptised, every one of you, in the name of Jesus Christ for the forgiveness of your sins. And you will receive the gift of the Holy Spirit. [39]The promise is for you and your children and for all who are far off – for all whom the Lord our God will call' (Acts 2:38b-39)

The question at the beginning of the church's on the day of Pentecost was not simply 'Do *in* Jesus?' but '*What* do you believe *about* Je clear, Peter says, as he stands up to addres Pentecost is that the evidence all points – to Jesus being *the Christ*. And if about that, then as you repent, ac' be the Lord and Christ, you can expect to receive the forgiveness of sins and the gift of the Holy Spirit. This remains true for us today. Jesus is both the Lord, to whom we are to submit, and the Christ who – by the forgiveness of our sins and the gift of the Holy Spirit – can save us.

Earlier we saw that 'turning' and 'trusting' can't be separated, ultimately because they are both signs of the Holy Spirit bringing a person to new birth, and the Holy Spirit will not leave his work half done. So, once again, it needs saying that these two steps, 'repenting' and 'receiving' (just different words to describe those same realities of 'turning' and 'trusting'), cannot be separated.

The Lord who rules and the Saviour who rescues come together in the one person, the Lord Jesus Christ. Inevitably in an explanation of what Christians believe, some Christians appear to stress the rule of Jesus and others the rescue of Jesus. But in reality they belong together and each informs the other.

So the only reason Christ can rescue us is because he rules. Jesus spoke of his superior power to bind the forces of darkness, and thereby to liberate us from the kingdom of darkness and bring us into the Kingdom of God.[5] Equally, it is true that the way Christ's rule is established in our lives is by bringing us his rescue – through the forgiveness of sins and the Holy Spirit given to God's forgiven people.

These two words, 'repent' and 'receive', are the key words that identify how lives are changed by Jesus. These words appeal to our *will*, but they do not bypass ꞁe appeal that Peter in his talk addresses to the *mind*; ᱟ need first to be convinced in our minds by the ᴛh about Jesus. Nor do these words bypass the

---

ꞁark 3:23-30

heart; we need to know in our hearts that we have done wrong and to be asking 'what shall we do?' But, for convinced minds and hearts stricken by a real sense of wrong, these two words – 'repent' and 'receive' – are at the heart of Peter's message that will change a human life. It was with these words, and many others like them, that the apostle Peter 'warned them; and he pleaded with them, "Save yourselves from this corrupt generation"'(Acts 2:40).

The effect of Peter's message addressed to mind, heart and will was electric and life-changing. Dr Luke, the writer, concludes:

> Those who accepted his message were baptised, and about three thousand were added to their number that day. (Acts 2:41)

The way that these three thousand or so individuals responded to Peter's message as he intended, is summarised in the words: (a) acceptance; (b) baptism and (c) community.

(A) ACCEPTANCE
'Those who accepted his message...'
To 'accept' the message about Jesus is really shorthand for understanding the message about Jesus with our minds, wanting him to save us in our hearts, and turning to him to receive from him with our lives.

The message is, therefore, life-changing as it work, first convincing my mind, second 'convi of wrong in my heart, and thirdly calling me and trust in Jesus (and specifically in his salvation) with my life.

That then is the question for eac will I, accept the message? All ove more than two thousand years, individuals who have been convinced in mind and heart by the truth of what Christians believe have turned to Jesus, making real for themselves what is made available for all. Reader, you will want to consider whether you could pray a prayer like this:

> *Lord God, I believe you are the maker of this world; you have made me to know you and to honour you with my life.*
>
> *I have turned away from you. I have neither submitted to your will for my life nor served my neighbours as I ought, and I am deserving of your judgment.*
>
> *You have sent your Son, Jesus Christ, to this world. He has lived the life I should have lived. He has suffered the death I deserved to die.*
>
> *I believe that you call me now to turn to Jesus to be the Lord of my life, and trust in Jesus to be my Saviour from judgment.*
>
> *As I repent now, I thank you for the promise you make that you will give to me the forgiveness of all my sins, and the gift of your Holy Spirit.*
>
> *Thank you…*

Some such prayer as this is not a magic mantra, but it will be the rough shape of a sincere communication with God. He will hear this prayer, and he has promised to answer it. 'The promise is for you and your children and for all who are far off – for all whom the Lord our God will call' (Acts 2:39).

3) BAPTISM

were baptised…'

ìtism does not itself accomplish our salvation, but to accompany it. Jesus himself commanded his vers:

> 'Go and make disciples of all nations, baptising them in the name of the Father and of the Son and of the Holy Spirit...' (Matt. 28:19)

It is, therefore, entirely in keeping with Christ's command that those who accepted Peter's message were baptised, just as believers are baptised today. And, in the experience of Christians, this act of obedience to Christ strengthens the convictions of those who turn to Christ. But what convictions does baptism symbolise? There are two possible answers.

First, *baptism can signify a burial*. When a person turns to Christ in repentance, the life they have lived for self, rather than for Christ, comes to an end. A person immersed in water at their baptism is, therefore, undergoing a burial. Bringing that same person up out of the water symbolises a resurrection to new life, a new life to be lived for Christ. This seems to be the thinking behind Paul's words:

> We were therefore buried with him through baptism into death in order that, just as Christ was raised from the dead through the glory of the Father, we too may live a new life. (Rom. 6:4)

In over twenty centuries of the Christian church, since the day of Pentecost when Peter preached, believers have often thought it appropriate to have their children baptised (or 'Christened', as it is sometimes called), on the basis that they will be brought up as Christians, both believing and obeying Jesus. That being so, it is possible that a person may consciously turn and trust in Christ as a child, a teenager or in adult life, only to discover he or she has already been baptised. Should such a person be baptised at this point? Some churches will not allow a further baptism at this point, whilst others may nearly insist on it! It is an issue on which Christians disagree, and there are some good arguments on both sides of the debate.

Secondly, *baptism symbolises a washing.* When a person turns to Christ, their life is 'washed clean', in the sense that the sin is washed away and God no longer sees the 'dirt'. There is no magic here; it is simply that God promises to forgive those who turn to Jesus and trust in his sin-bearing death. Baptism with water is a visual aid of the stain of sin washed away. This seems to be the thinking behind Paul's words:

> ...Christ loved the church and gave himself up for her [26]to make her holy, cleansing her by the washing with water through the word, [27]and to present her to himself as a radiant church, without stain or wrinkle or any other blemish, but holy and blameless. (Eph. 5:25b-27)

That phrase *'washing with water through the word'* refers to the fact that Jesus' word *promises* forgiveness, and the water of baptism *symbolises* it.

(C) COMMUNITY
'...and about three thousand were added to their number that day'.

For some of us this detail will be a surprising note on which to end, and a strange conclusion to Luke's account of Peter's preaching on the day of Pentecost. We might assume that what is so intensely personal (a person's restored relationship with God), might be expressed just privately. But in fact that is not so; my personal commitment to Christ is to find expression in a public commitment to God's people. Luke records something of the common life of God's people in Jerusalem at that time:

> They devoted themselves to the apostles' teaching
> and to the fellowship, to the breaking of bread and to
> prayer. (Acts 2:42)

This is not something arbitrary that I add to the saving work of Christ on the cross. No, when I come to belong to God, through Christ, I come to belong also to God's people. That is a wonderful truth which will find expression in my identification with a local fellowship of God's people. And in that fellowship I will look to serve, and be served by, other Christians. Any faithful fellowship of God's people will look to reflect three core activities of this gathering of Christians in Jerusalem.

The first is a devotion to the apostles' teaching, on the basis that their word (which we now have in the Bible) has brought me to life in Christ and will further strengthen and establish that new life.

The second is a commitment to one another's well-being. In the verses that follow we read, 'All the believers were together and had everything in common' (Acts 2:44). That may look different in different cultures and communities at different times, but it will extend in various ways to opening our hearts and homes to one another, and to sharing meals and possessions.

The third core activity in the life of a fellowship will be engaging with God in prayer and praise, and specifically in celebrating God's provision for his people in the death of his Son.

Once a person trusts in Jesus' death for their life, and turns to him as their Lord, life will never quite be the same again; the man we look at in the following chapter will illustrate that. Acceptance of the message, baptism in the name of Jesus Christ, and the alignment or identification of my life with that of a community of God's people will signal a new start to a new life with a new purpose. I will discover, increasingly, the joy of knowing and serving God for which he made me, and saved me through his Son.

9 A real-life story

We've looked at the principle; but what about the practice? How does the truth of *what Christians believe* actually save and change a life? Every believer in Jesus will have a real-life story of how encountering Jesus has saved and changed, and continues to shape their life. I look back to a period in 1977 when the message of God's care for a wayward world came home to me as an individual with peculiar force and clarity. For others the precise occasion of the 'new birth' is not dateable, but the fact of being alive to God is no less real.

Of course the changes don't come all at once but it's a bit like a house coming under new ownership. Some changes take place quite quickly; a different car in the driveway, new faces occupying the house, a different set of friends and relations who visit, and so on. But, more than that, the fact of a new owner signals that a great deal will change in the years that follow: new kitchens, bathrooms, windows, carpets and the rest.

Therefore, we mustn't be impatient about the pace of change in our lives; once we come under the ownership of the Lord Jesus Christ, the change starts – and it doesn't stop, but it is not all done and dusted there and then. The believer remains a 'work in progress'. John Newton, the one-time slave trader who himself became a Christian, said, 'I am not the man I ought to be, I am not the man I wish to be, and I am not the man I hope to be, but by the grace of God, I am not the man I used to be.'[1]

The key is to make a start with Jesus. For God's offer to us of new life in Christ is of no value until it is taken up. Christianity is about responding to God's invitation and entering into a personal relationship with him. To understand how this happens, we are going to look at the account of one man – recorded in Luke's Gospel – who came to new life in Christ.

> [1]Jesus entered Jericho and was passing through. [2]A man was there by the name of Zacchaeus; he was a chief tax collector and was wealthy. [3]He wanted to see who Jesus was, but being a short man he could not, because of the crowd. [4]So he ran ahead and climbed a sycamore-fig tree to see him, since Jesus was coming that way.
>
> [5]When Jesus reached the spot, he looked up and said to him, 'Zacchaeus, come down immediately. I must stay at your house today.' [6]So he came down at once and welcomed him gladly.
>
> [7]All the people saw this and began to mutter, 'He has gone to be the guest of a "sinner".'

---

1   This is a paraphrase of the fuller quotation: 'I am not what I ought to be — ah, how imperfect and deficient! I am not what I wish to be — I abhor what is evil, and I would cleave to what is good! I am not what I hope to be — soon, soon shall I put off mortality, and with mortality all sin and imperfection. Yet, though I am not what I ought to be, nor what I wish to be, nor what I hope to be, I can truly say, I am not what I once was; a slave to sin and Satan; and I can heartily join with the apostle, and acknowledge, "By the grace of God I am what I am." ' As quoted in *The Christian Pioneer* (1856) edited by Joseph Foulkes Winks, p. 84.

[8]But Zacchaeus stood up and said to the Lord, 'Look, Lord! Here and now I give half of my possessions to the poor, and if I have cheated anybody out of anything, I will pay back four times the amount.'
[9]Jesus said to him, 'Today salvation has come to this house, because this man, too, is a Son of Abraham. [10]For the Son of Man came to seek and to save what was lost.' (Luke 19:1-10)

Children's Bibles can go to town on the picture of this little man, this wealthy man, perhaps this rather portly man, up a tree looking over the heads of the crowds for Jesus who was coming his way.

However, the pictures struggle to convey the really significant truths about Zacchaeus, told us here by Luke, which are not to do so much with his physical stature as his social and spiritual standing. We are told by Luke that he is a 'chief tax collector' and that his compatriots identify him as 'a sinner'.

For most of us these would be entirely disconnected thoughts; 'tax collector' being a job description, 'sinner' being a moral or spiritual character assessment. But that simply reflects that, for us, 'social' and 'spiritual' issues come in quite separate baskets, whereas for the Jews of Jesus' day these could be linked.

The category of 'tax collector' identified those whose way of life alienated them from God's people. For the Jewish people of Jesus' day there was no society that mattered other than the society of *God's* people, so to be a social outcast was to be a spiritual reject (a 'sinner') too.

And Zacchaeus was a social outcast, for the twin reasons that he was both a traitor and a trickster. He was a traitor because he was a tax collector in the employ of the occupying enemy, the Romans, who were colonizing Jerusalem. And he was a trickster because almost certainly he would have made his wealth from dishonestly collecting surplus amounts of tax, and pocketing these for himself.

So, in brief, this twin description of Zacchaeus as a tax collector and sinner identify him both as a social outcast and a spiritual reject. Materially he was a wealthy man, but spiritually he was a poor man and an isolated individual in Israel. These are the colours that are easy to see in Luke's brief description of this man, albeit they would be hard to paint on a canvas.

Why does Luke record this man's encounter with Jesus? He is nothing like the many poor 'down-and-outs' that Jesus regularly encountered – as, for example, the nameless and blind beggar whom Luke records in earlier verses. It may be precisely because of this apparent contrast that Luke includes this encounter. The down-and-out have great needs; the 'up-and-out' also. But with this difference: the blind beggar knows his need and cries out, 'have mercy on me', whereas those of us who are materially satisfied may not be so conscious of our spiritual need.

Zacchaeus discreetly climbs a tree; he is curious to see Jesus, but as far as we know there is no real consciousness of need in this self-made and self-sufficient man. We may be the same. Few of us will see ourselves as wealthy, and in one sense it is a rather arbitrary description. What is 'wealthy'? It all depends on those with whom we are comparing ourselves. But, like Zacchaeus, it may be the case that even the modest resources we think we have can be spiritually blinding. Money will tend to buy me comfort in this life, and limit my horizons to the span of time I am here on earth to enjoy it.

Saying to myself, 'You have plenty of good things laid up for many years... take life easy; eat, drink and be merry' (Luke 12:13-21) is a foolish and potentially fatal attitude; it confuses material provision with spiritual provision. But the one is not equivalent to the other; indeed there is no rate of exchange to convert the one to the other. Jesus says, 'What good is it for a man to gain the whole world, yet forfeit his soul?' (Mark 8:36-37). He is warning it is sadly possible to gain this world and lose the next.

So while a wealthy man has the spiritual needs that all men have, he may well labour under the illusion that because all is well with him materially speaking, all is well with him and God spiritually speaking. Such a man is Zacchaeus, and we may have much in common with him. It is that situation of spiritual need, fatally concealed, that Jesus encounters and transforms.

CHRIST'S CALL

The single most astonishing truth taught us through the encounter between Jesus and Zacchaeus is that Jesus takes the initiative to come to Zacchaeus' house:

> [5]When Jesus reached the spot, he looked up and said to him, 'Zacchaeus, come down immediately. I must stay at your house today.' [6]So he came down at once and welcomed him gladly. [7]All the people saw this and began to mutter, 'He has gone to be the guest of a "sinner".' (Luke 19:5-7)

We may feel that Zacchaeus, who is scorned by his self-righteous countrymen, is really only getting from Jesus the fairer and more favourable attention that he actually deserves. But however much we are drawn to the underdog, or inclined to side with the outsider, we mustn't rewrite the script and miss the point, which is that Zacchaeus deserves nothing from Jesus.

The truth remains that he has been dishonest with money, and that he has been more driven by the pursuit of money than a principled love for God and God's people. Of course he is not alone in this, but neither can he escape the truth of the observation that he is a sinner. To put it another way, he, like all of us, is in need of salvation. It's a salvation that is needed at three levels.

First, I need saving from a fatal separation from God.
This is a shock. God is my maker and I may reason there can be no gulf between us. But there is; I have rebelled against him; I am deserving of his judgment and even whilst the fullness of that judgment is suspended, my sin separates me from God, so that I am out of relationship with him:

> Your iniquities have separated you from your God; your sins have hidden his face from you, so that he will not hear. (Isa. 59:2)

As in the parables earlier in Luke's Gospel (Luke 15), of the lost sheep, the lost coin and the lost son, I am 'lost to God'. I am both estranged from him now, and in danger of his judgment to come, which threatens to bring me an eternal separation from God in the future. I need saving from this estrangement from God.

Second, I need saving from my isolation from God's people.
We are made for a relationship with God, but if I am out of relationship with God, I am out of relationship with the people of God. I might meet with God's people (as a churchgoer), and know the people who know their God, but if I am lost to God I do not *belong* to God's people. That was the case for Zacchaeus. Perhaps for him this was the most obvious aspect of his spiritual lostness. He simply did not belong, and he needed to be restored to fellowship with the people of God.

Third, I need saving from myself.
Sin is not just a surface blemish on our character; it is a deep-seated sickness in our soul. We do not simply need a good scrub to make us clean and presentable on the outside; we need a cure for the disease which is on the inside. Many of the mechanisms we have for making ourselves presentable in front of the world around us leave us unchanged in our innermost being. Good education, good manners, good housing, good rest, even good exercise and good diet, will all help to make us present well. But none of these is a remedy for the sickness of sin which means that my heart is fundamentally inclined away from a love for God and for other people.

Without salvation, I am the centre of my own world even if I can, by the gathering of information and a process of education, expand my horizons. I need, as has been said, to 'be saved from the dark, dirty little dungeon of my own ego.'[2] Zacchaeus needed this change of heart. He could not by himself change himself. I, too, need to be saved from myself.

Here, then, is Zacchaeus, indeed everyone by nature, lost and needing to be saved from God-forsakenness, separation from God's people, and captivity to sinful, selfish self. And now Christ sees him up a tree, and calls him with what must have been an unforgettable invitation, 'Zacchaeus, come down immediately. I must stay at your house today' (v. 5).

This call of Christ is something more significant, of course, than someone simply inviting himself round for a meal. The Pharisees and teachers of the law have earlier observed that 'this man [Jesus] welcomes sinners and eats with them' (Luke 15:2). Here is the sinless Son

---

2   Attributed to Malcolm Muggeridge.

of God at the home of a sinner. It's a very significant gesture, as the onlookers of these events know, in that it symbolises acceptance or fellowship despite the sins of his host. And, more than that, for the Son of God to do this symbolises the forgiveness of sins.

By gracious deed, if not yet by explicit word, Jesus is demonstrating that he himself can bridge the two otherwise unbridgeable gulfs that exist for Zacchaeus, as they exist for us all: the first is the gulf between man and God; the second is the gulf between us and the people of God. Elsewhere, this is summarised as being 'without God in the world' and 'excluded from citizenship in Israel' (Eph. 2:11-22). We may say Jesus is effecting a double reconciliation in place of a double alienation.

And this double reconciliation comes not because Zacchaeus is a champion tree-climber, or in some other way deserving of Christ's attention and salvation. Christ is in the home of Zacchaeus, with all the significance that carries, because of the initiative that Jesus here takes: 'Zacchaeus, come down immediately. I must stay at your house today.'

What is being graphically illustrated here in this encounter is what the Bible calls *'grace'*. The word speaks of God's *initiative* towards *undeserving* people. Both aspects are significant. First, grace speaks of God's initiative. God makes the first move with us; he does not wait for us to move towards him. Secondly, grace speaks of God giving generously to undeserving people. So the crowds mutter, 'He has gone to be the guest of a "sinner."' Zacchaeus was indeed one such undeserving person; I am another and, reader, you are another.

That initiative of the grace of God to save a person becomes evident in the change of mind and heart in an individual. This change – possible thanks only to God himself – is sometimes described as a conversion.

ZACCHAEUS' CONVERSION

The work of Christ is a hidden work in the heart of any man, woman or child. But, as we saw with Nicodemus (ch. 7), even if God's work by his Spirit in the heart of any man is an invisible work, the *effects* of that work soon become apparent. The wind may come from we don't know where, and go we know not where, but we can see where the wind has blown; it shakes the branches on the trees. We turn then from Christ's more or less invisible work in the heart of Zacchaeus to its visible outworking in Zacchaeus' life.

> [8]But Zacchaeus stood up and said to the Lord, 'Look, Lord! Here and now I give half of my possessions to the poor, and if I have cheated anybody out of anything, I will pay back four times the amount.'
>
> [9]Jesus said to him, 'Today salvation has come to this house, because this man, too, is a son of Abraham. [10]For the Son of Man came to seek and to save what was lost.' (Luke 19:8-10)

The immediate change in Zacchaeus' life is his gladness, but more specifically we can identify three glad gestures.

A glad welcome
'So he came down at once and welcomed him gladly' (v. 6).

In the four Gospels, the primary focus is on Jesus revealing himself, both who he is and what he has come to do. But a good deal of attention is paid also to the *response* that people make to Jesus. He is sometimes rejected, often indeed by the religious leaders. He is frequently misunderstood by the crowds. And then there are those who hear him, understand him and receive him. Clearly, Zacchaeus is one such man.

For Luke is surely telling us here that the one who opened the door of his home to Jesus 'to welcome him warmly', was enabled to open the door of his heart to him also. Zacchaeus' hospitality shown to Jesus was all of a piece with a heart response to Jesus; it was a sign that Jesus' message of himself as Lord and Christ, as Saviour and King, had taken root in Zacchaeus' life. '*He came down at once and welcomed him warmly*'.

A glad repentance

'*...if I have cheated anybody out of anything, I will pay back four times the amount*' (v. 8).

Money is important to many of us, and certainly Zacchaeus was no exception. Zacchaeus' wealth didn't in any way make him deserving of Jesus' attention. Nor did it somehow put Zacchaeus in the 'too hard to save' or 'too unlovely to love' category; indeed there is no such category for the Saviour of sinners. Money didn't earn him favour; it didn't disqualify him from receiving the gift of salvation either. But Zacchaeus' attitude to money was always going to be an indicator of the state of his heart. If Jesus had changed his heart, it was in his attitude to money that it would be most obvious.

And in two ways it becomes apparent. The first is that he desires to compensate those he has cheated. 'If I have cheated anybody out of anything, I will pay back four times the amount' (v. 8). To receive Jesus is to receive him for who he is, namely the Lord of this world, and the rightful ruler of my life. That means Jesus leads us forward for the future rather than that he puts the clock back for us. That being so, not all my past wrongs can be righted. But some can! And the sign that Jesus is Lord of my future is that I put right what I can. Some relationships that I have damaged can be repaired. Some goods stolen can be returned. It is a significant sign that Jesus is now Zacchaeus' Lord that Zacchaeus volunteers to return what he has gained by dishonesty.

There is a second way in which Zacchaeus' handling of his money makes evident the change in his heart.

A glad deliverance

'Look, Lord! Here and now I give half of my possessions to the poor...' (v. 8).

Repentance was evidenced by restitution, as we have seen. But making restitution of stolen money would only be one aspect of submission to Jesus' lordship. It was putting right what he should not have done wrong. Rules and laws are good at showing us what we are *not* to do. Eight of the 'Ten Commandments' themselves are framed as prohibitions, including the eighth commandment, 'you shall not steal', which Zacchaeus here acknowledged he has not kept.

But there are sins of omission as well as commission. We fail to live as God intends by failing to do what he commands every bit as much as by doing what he prohibits. And for Zacchaeus there was not only a restitution of stolen money to be made, but also deliverance from the grip of money to be experienced. For the essence of God's law is love for God: 'Love the Lord your God with all your heart and with all your soul and with all your mind...' and as Jesus taught on another occasion, 'You cannot serve both God and Money' (Matt. 22:37-39; 6:24) – for 'serving money' is an aspect of serving self.

Salvation, however, is in part being delivered from the love and service of self. Love of self, it has been said, 'is a stolen love.'[3] But it is gripping. And to be delivered from

---

3   '...Love of self is a stolen love. It was destined for others; they needed it to live, to thrive, and I have diverted it.' From a prayer by Michel Quoist, French writer (1921-1997).

its grasp, I need what another has called 'the expulsive power of a new affection'.[4] When Christ calls me, making known his grace to forgive me my sins, to reconcile me to himself and to include me among his people, my heart will experience the wonder of that love for him and for others that will begin to undo that love of self.

The evidence is that Zacchaeus experiences just such a deliverance. How so? This inveterate 'go-getter' becomes a glad and generous giver; 'Look, Lord! Here and now I give half of my possessions to the poor…'(v. 8). His heart has been turned to keep the heart of God's law of love.

A cynic might imagine that the best explanation for this is that Zacchaeus realised the game was up. That it was payback time for a greedy man. That he had met in Jesus the judge of all men, and that he was doing his best to divest himself of the riches that would witness against him in the heavenly courtroom. But it would be more accurate to read out of this encounter not merely the prospect of judgment, but the promise of mercy. And to see that what broke the love of money and the love of self was not a vain attempt at self-justification, but a glad appreciation of the justification given to him by the sheer mercy of God, shown in his Son.

Christians often speak of 'the cost of discipleship', because, of course, Jesus did too.[5] And it is clear that for Zacchaeus to follow Christ there was a price to pay in so far as from now on there was a different life to be lived.

But this account of Zacchaeus' encounter with Jesus clarifies that the price we pay is not the cost of earning the right to be called disciples, so much as the

---

4   Title of a sermon by Thomas Chalmers, Scottish pastor / teacher (1780-1847).

5   e.g. Luke 9:21-27; 14:25-35.

happy *consequence* in our lives of being liberated by Jesus from the grip of sin and self. One man from a Hindu background, who subsequently came to put his trust in Christ, put it this way:

> I wanted to belong to God so much that in my heart I was willing to pay any price. This is what it actually cost me. Imagine I came to your house with a kidney machine to sell when you are on the point of dying through kidney failure and you enquire how much it costs. If my reply is that I will exchange it for the rubbish in your back garden, would you consider it too great a price to pay? Wouldn't you be only too willing to pay any price for that machine? The cost I had to pay Jesus was the rubbish in my back garden; my sin, my selfish nature, all that made me unhappy and made my life a misery. I could have cherished my rubbish and said 'no' to him as some people do, but that thought never even crossed my mind.[6]

It is as though Jesus says to us, 'Will you let me take the rubbish in your life to the tip?' Some of us will be able to recall agonies of indecision as we loaded up the car to go to the tip. Perhaps one member of the family wanted to chuck out something that another thought should be kept –'it could be useful one day', and so on. But almost never do we live to regret the things we take to the tip, however difficult a decision it was at the time to let them go.

And it is the same with the 'rubbish removal' Jesus undertakes for us. Yes, from one vantage point there is a cost. This selfish habit will have to go, and that unworthy ambition; this idol and that obsession. But what endures is delight at the freedom from those things which, in retrospect, were worthless clutter – things

---

6   From *Only One God,* by Vijay Menon.

which would certainly spoil the enjoyment of friendship with the Lord Jesus Christ.

Here, then, are the signs of a man found by the mercy of God in Christ, and by that mercy made a follower of Christ. He gave a *glad welcome* to Jesus, the man and his message. He displayed a heart newly and *gladly repent-ant*, acknowledging his wrong. And he gave convincing testimony of a *glad deliverance* from the power of sin and self for the love of God and neighbour.

It seems Zacchaeus was at every point so glad to be turning to Christ that he had little need to be turned to God by the prospect of the judgment of God on impenitence and unbelief. We ought not to conclude, however, that a life turned to God by the prospect of his judgment is less genuine than a life turned to God by the promise of mercy. Both are essential truths about God, and he knows my heart and how to turn it to himself. I am no less genuinely turned by God to himself at the message of his wrath than I am by the message of his mercy.

But most of us will need both the warning of judgment and the message of mercy. If I fear judgment, without knowing mercy, I shall experience no glad deliverance. Equally, if I hear of mercy without believing in judgment, it will make no sense and answer no real need. God's way encompasses both. The one-time slave trader who himself became a Christian, John Newton, expressed it in his hymn *Amazing Grace,*

> 'Twas Grace that taught my heart to fear,
> And Grace my fears relieved;
> How precious did that Grace appear
> The hour I first believed.

The reason why 'grace' was precious to Newton was because the prospect of God's judgment was real too.

And probably for Zacchaeus also, there was a deliverance brought about both by a right fear of a judge, and also by the right adoration of a Saviour. Of this man, Jesus was able to say the wonderful words, 'Today salvation has come to this house ...' (v. 9).

What Christians believe is that God, through his Son, seeks, finds and saves those who are lost. Christ's call and Zacchaeus' conversion show us that. But Jesus' own gloss on this encounter with Zacchaeus is that this life saved and turned to God is itself to be seen as part of a bigger picture on a larger canvas concerning God's promise of a family for Abraham.

Abraham's family

> ⁹Jesus said to him, 'Today salvation has come to this house, because this man, too, is a son of Abraham. ¹⁰For the Son of Man came to seek and to save what was lost.' (Luke 19:9-10)

It would perhaps be a surprise to many of us found by the Son of Man to know that we too are described as 'sons of Abraham'. But that title indicates both God's ultimate purpose and a Christian's true identity.

Jesus' ultimate purpose

Jesus has come to seek and to save what was lost. But his task is not completed by bringing sinners back to God, though that is essential and foundational. A fuller description of his purpose would be that he came to fulfil the promise made in history to a man called Abraham, to provide Abraham with children:

> ⁴Then the word of the LORD came to him... 'Look up at the heavens and count the stars – if indeed you can count them.' Then he said to him, 'So shall your offspring be.' (Gen. 15:4-5)

The promise that God here made to Abraham is the promise that God works to fulfil through history. And it is fulfilled both through individuals being brought back into relationship with their maker, and through those same individuals being made part of the family of Abraham.

To belong to the family of Abraham is not a matter of being descended physically from Abraham. Indeed, the Bible is clear it requires not physical descent (from Abraham) but spiritual birth (by the Spirit of God) to make me a member of that family.

The sign of that work of the Spirit of God in a person's life is that she or he is brought to believe in Jesus, and the message of redemption through his sin-bearing death on a cross. And that means that the family of Abraham is composed of *all* (and not just 'Jewish') believers in Jesus:

> [7]Understand, then, that those who believe are children of Abraham.

> [26]You are all sons of God through faith in Christ Jesus, [27]for all of you who were baptised into Christ have clothed yourselves with Christ. [28]There is neither Jew nor Greek, slave nor free, male nor female, for you are all one in Christ Jesus. [29]If you belong to Christ, then you are Abraham's seed, and heirs according to the promise. (Gal. 3:7, 26-29)

Zacchaeus is one such man to whom Jesus can say 'Today salvation has come to this house, because this man, too, is a son of Abraham' (v. 9): a person saved by Christ Jesus, *is* a son of Abraham.

God's purpose in history is the fulfilment of the promise made to Abraham, of a vast family. Every believer in Jesus is part of the fulfilment of that promise.

A Christian's clearer identity

Understanding God's purpose in history also clarifies the Christian's identity. It means that if the Spirit brings me to new birth, I am brought to belong both to God, and to God's people.

To belong to God makes me a child of God. And the Spirit of God exercises a continuing ministry in the lives of believers, to assure us of this. The apostle Paul writes, 'The Spirit himself testifies with our spirit that we are God's children' (Rom. 8:16).

To belong to the people of God makes me a son of Abraham. This was the assurance given to Zacchaeus: 'Today salvation has come to this house, because this man, too, is a son of Abraham' (v. 9).

This was for Zacchaeus an authoritative and official ending of his separation from the people of God. He had it on no less an authority than that of the Son of God that he, Zacchaeus, belonged to the people of God.

And the same is true for each person made new by God's Spirit today; he or she becomes a son of Abraham. It means I belong to the one people of God which, since Abraham, God has been establishing through history. It is my privilege to live out that membership of the people of God all my life.

It means that God intends me to belong to a fellowship of God's people in which I can love and be loved, serve and be served. The particular fellowship – or church – to which I belong, is the environment in which God intends that I grow to maturity as a Christian, something I cannot do on my own. The moment I turn and trust in Christ, I am like a newborn baby. There follows the opportunity for growth in my knowledge and love of God which is to last as long as I live. The fellowship to which I belong will be home, family, school and opportunity for service.

****

If you have heard Christ's call, and turned to trust and to follow him, God has received you as a child into his family and there are Christians ready to welcome you into Abraham's family!

It may be you are not as yet in that position. Note then that Jesus' last word is not about Zacchaeus, saved to belong to God and to God's people. It is about himself: *'For the Son of Han came to seek and to save what was lost'* (Luke 19:10).

At its heart the Christian faith is about Jesus, the Son of God whom the Father has sent to live, and supremely to die, and then to rise from the dead, to save lost people. That's what Christians believe, and the Christian faith can only be described by such truths affirmed in the Bible that we have looked at briefly in these pages.

So the Son of Man came not just to teach me but to seek me; not just to sympathise with the lost but to save us. Of course, simply *knowing* what Christians believe is of little value. This knowledge, rightly understood, is just a means to the end of enjoying the salvation Jesus came to bring. When I turn to Jesus and trust in him personally, asking that the Lord of this world be *my* Lord, and that the Saviour of the world be *my* Saviour, then believing *what Christians believe* has accomplished what the Son of Man came to this world to do.

Postscript

I promised a short postscript on the critical assumption of this book that *the Bible is reliable in all that it teaches*. I am not at this point trying to persuade anyone of something they think is untrue. If the message of the Bible we have been looking at has not seemed convincing, these last few pages will not be what make the difference. But someone may, for the sake of completeness, want to ask whether believing the Bible is akin to intellectual suicide. The answer is 'no, it is not.'

In many different ways, the Bible testifies to its own reliability and truthfulness. For example, the apostle Paul writes to Timothy:

> All Scripture is God-breathed and is useful for teaching, rebuking, correcting and training in righteousness, so that the man of God may be thoroughly equipped for every good work. (2 Tim. 3:16)

There is, of course, circularity about the argument that looks to the Bible (of whose reliability we wish to be assured) for evidence that the Bible is reliable. But where else can we look to establish such a claim? If another 'God-given' text exists which establishes the truth of the Bible's claim to be reliable, well we could go there. But the same question would need to be asked of *that* text; how can we be sure *that* text is reliable? It is a never-ending quest for an ultimate and unquestionably reliable authority.

Granted then that accepting the Bible's testimony to itself is a circular argument, is it nonetheless a reasonable testimony to receive and believe? Christians believe it is, principally because of the answers which can be given to the following three questions.

1. Can we be sure our Bible contains what the authors of Scripture wrote?

We do not have any of the original parchments or manuscripts for any part of the Bible. In common with other ancient documents, therefore, the accuracy of our text today depends on (a) the number of manuscripts we have (copies of the original, or copies of copies), and (b) the nearness in time of the date of the copies to the writing of the originals.

On the basis of the answers to these two questions, we can conclude that the documentary evidence for the accuracy of the New Testament documents is very strong. There are a number of books that address this issue.[1]

2. But, even if we have good documentary evidence, can we be sure that those who recorded his words and deeds did so accurately?

Even assuming we have what the authors of the Gospels wrote (Matthew, Mark, Luke and John), can we be sure that what the authors of the Gospels wrote was actually an accurate recording of what was said and done?

There are at least three reasons to think so. First, the disciples purport to convey some of the most exalted

---

1   For example, *Are the New Testament documents reliable?*, by F.F. Bruce, and
     Is the New Testament History?, by Paul Barnett.

moral and ethical teaching the world has ever known from the lips of God himself. It seems likely that they would have set about doing this carefully.

Second, it is clear that *someone* said the things attributed to Jesus – because they exist in print in front of us – and whoever did so was a gigantic human figure in history. It seems easiest to believe that these words attributed to Jesus were indeed spoken by such a one as performed the miracles, and made the claims attributed to him.

There is a third reason to believe that the record of the Gospel writers is reliable, which is that they record the resurrection of Jesus from the dead. They claimed to have encountered the risen Jesus and witnessed the empty tomb. If these things are not true, and Jesus did not rise from the dead, then either the first Christians were totally deceived or totally deceptive. The former seems incredible;[2] the latter involves the psychologically implausible phenomenon of many of the first Christian disciples being willing to die for what they knew was a lie. On the other hand, if this is accurate reporting, and Jesus did actually rise again from the dead, then it is hard to know why we would stumble to believe the rest of the biblical record which contains nothing harder to believe.

3. Did Jesus teach the truth?

Assuming we have what the New Testament authors wrote (question 1), and that they accurately reported what they witnessed (question 2), the third question concerns Jesus of whom they speak. Certainly he made enormous claims for himself as the one who has come

---

2   Sir Norman Anderson's *Evidence for the Resurrection,* referred to in chapter 4, addresses the possibility that the disciples were deluded.

from the presence of God,[3] and indeed to be God dwelling among us.[4] But was Jesus telling the truth?

If he was not telling the truth, we would need to decide whether that was because he was being deliberately deceptive or because he was himself deceived as to his own identity. Both these options are hard to believe. As to the first, is it likely that the one who himself taught the highest of moral standards was himself a self-obsessed liar? As to the second option, this was clearly canvassed by some of Jesus' enemies,[5] but the combination of wisdom and love, and the evident sanity with which he spoke, do not lead one to believe that he was deranged. If, then, Jesus was neither a bad man nor a mad man, we are left with the option which does indeed commend itself to Christians, namely that he told the truth about himself, and that he was the God-man.

Many of the questions people raise about the Bible fall into the categories above. Do we have what the authors of Scripture wrote? If so, did the authors of Scripture accurately report what they saw and heard? And if so, was Jesus who he actually claimed to be? The harder question, however, is the question which Jesus asks of us. He asks not just, 'Can you believe?' but rather, 'Will you receive me as your Lord and Saviour?'

> [10]He was in the world, and though the world was made through him, the world did not recognise him. [11]He came to that which was his own, but his own did not receive him. [12]Yet to all who received him, to those who believed in his name, he gave the right to become children of God – [13]children born not of natural descent, nor of human decision or a husband's will, but born of God. (John 1:10-13)

---

3   'If God were your Father, you would love me, for I came from God and now am here. I have not come on my own; but he sent me' (John 8:42).

4   'We are not stoning you for any of these [great miracles], but for blasphemy, because you, a mere man, claim to be God' (John 8:33).

5   'At these words the Jews were again divided. Many of them said, "He is demon-possessed and raving mad. Why listen to him?" But others said, "These are not the sayings of a man possessed by a demon. Can a demon open the eyes of the blind?"' (John 10:19-21).

Abbreviations

In this book, the following books from the Bible are referenced. When in parentheses, these abbreviations are used.

Old Testament

Genesis	Gen.	1 Chronicles	1 Chron.
Exodus	Exod.	2 Chronicles	2 Chron.
Numbers	Num.	Psalms	Ps.
Deuteronomy	Deut.	Isaiah	Isa.
1 Samuel	1 Sam.		

New Testament

Matthew	Matt.	1 Thessalonians	1 Thess.
Romans	Rom.	1 Timothy	1 Tim.
1 Corinthians	1 Cor.	2 Timothy	2 Tim.
2 Corinthians	2 Cor.	Hebrews	Heb.
Galatians	Gal.	1 Peter	1 Pet.
Ephesians	Eph.	2 Peter	2 Pet.
Philippians	Phil.	Revelation	Rev.

Christian Focus Publications
publishes books for all ages

Our mission statement –

STAYING FAITHFUL
In dependence upon God we seek to impact the world through literature faithful to His infallible Word, the Bible. Our aim is to ensure that the Lord Jesus Christ is presented as the only hope to obtain forgiveness of sin, live a useful life and look forward to heaven with Him.

REACHING OUT
Christ's last command requires us to reach out to our world with His gospel. We seek to help fulfil that by publishing books that point people towards Jesus and help them develop a Christ-like maturity. We aim to equip all levels of readers for life, work, ministry and mission.

Books in our adult range are published in three imprints:

Christian Focus contains popular works including biographies, commentaries, basic doctrine and Christian living. Our children's books are also published in this imprint.

Mentor focuses on books written at a level suitable for Bible College and seminary students, pastors, and other serious readers. The imprint includes commentaries, doctrinal studies, examination of current issues and church history.

Christian Heritage contains classic writings from the past.

Christian Focus Publications Ltd,
Geanies House, Fearn, Ross-shire,
IV20 1TW, Scotland, United Kingdom.
www.christianfocus.com